Mexico City

AN OPINIONATED GUIDE
for the Curious Traveler

Jim Johnston

Book design: Romney Lange
www.creativedirect.com

Acknowledgements

I would like to thank Romney Lange, Daniel Barón, Veronica Moctezuma Rivera, Harriet and Irving Berg, Carol Romano, Valeria Clark, Beverly Donofrio, Tony Cohan, Janice Eidus, Rachel Wysoker, Jaime Montes, Barbara Luboff, Luisa Field, Rowena Galavitz, Regina Gomez Dantes, Angel Valtierra, Dolores Quintera, Patrice Wynne, Michael Parker Stainback, Masako Takahashi, Pauline Frommer, Louis and Elodie Santamaria, Suzanne Kimball (RIP), and Nicholas Gilman for their invaluable assistance in creating this book.

Torre Latinoamericana, Centro Histórico

Table of Contents

Introduction

When I tell people I live in Mexico City, the response is often bewilderment shadowed with trepidation. I've called Mexico City home since 1998: in that time I've seen it grow and change—mostly for the better. As one of the biggest conglomerations of human beings on the planet, its sheer size can be daunting, and everybody (especially those who have never been here) has a crime or a pollution story, the grittier the better. But as a resident explorer of the city for more than 15 years, I have come to know it well, to manage its complexities, to make it enjoyable, even delectable.

What started out as a collection of notes on my discoveries around town to share with friends has grown into this guide, a love letter to my home town, known here simply as Mexico, el DF (el day-effay), el Distrito Federal or, nowadays, CDMX (Ciudad de México). It's a biased book, I admit, rooted in a love that accepts many imperfections without overlooking them. I include a number of popular tourist sites that nobody should miss, but also lesser-known places, neighborhoods, markets, and even a specific street corner where you will find the best tamales. I don't give long descriptions of the most famous sights—I'll assume the curious traveler can figure that out—but I try to lead you into less likely corners. My opinions are colored by my professional life as an artist and architect, my interest in good food, and my love of great cities in general.

Mexico City isn't really beautiful like Paris or San Francisco—its gems lie in a matrix of urban hysteria. It can delight and assault the senses with equal force, then teasingly hide much of its allure behind massive old walls. With population estimates as high as 25 million, the tumult of noise and activity can be overwhelming, and the extremes of wealth and poverty unsettling. There is a great deal of sensory input and it takes some effort to sort it all out.

Unlike more demure European or American cities, Mexico pours out onto its streets with unrestrained exuberance. Color is everywhere: radiant magenta, acidic lime green, or screeching yellow will suddenly appear on a wall or a shirt, a balloon or a piece of fruit. Advertising is boldly painted directly on building walls, creating a delightful, if disorienting overabundance of visual information. Hand-hewn stones, irregular surfaces, and cobbled streets give the city an earthy physical

Polanco, Anthropology Museum

texture. Cracks, bumps, gaps, and tilting walls, evidence of many earthquakes, make the city seem like a child's drawing. And with zoning laws often ignored, startling juxtapositions occur: a stately colonial building looms over a 60's gas station, or a high-rise apartment complex cuddles up to a humble taco stand. It is the capital of the unexpected.

Mexico City has a great sound track, and I often stop to listen—it's a very musical country. Organ grinders wander about; it's an old tradition

Mercado Jamica

that arrived with Italian immigrants a century ago (give a tip—it's their only source of income). Singers accompany themselves with guitars and accordions in the streets, in restaurants and in the metro. Every so often a marimba band will appear on the sidewalk in front of my house. The 'One Man Band' is a regular in the neighborhood where I work, his crude fanfare for trumpet and drum guaranteed to wake you up from an afternoon slump. There's a surprising number of birds here, and on quiet holiday mornings I've been awakened by their song.

Market vendors have their particular calls and cadences (called *pregones*), knife sharpeners have their distinctive whistle (not to be confused with the whistle of the *camotero* who sells cooked sweet potatoes in the evening). Even the garbage collectors have a particular sound, the clanging of a metal bar, to announce their arrival. The recorded cries of *fiero viejo* (old junk metal) collectors, or "tamales Oaxaqueños", with their combination of humor and annoyance, are well-known to all residents of Mexico City. Many foreigners find the noise level unsettling, but volume and cacophony are more often experienced as pleasure than annoyance by Mexicans - visit Plaza Garibaldi one night to hear the mariachis and you will know what I mean.

The city smells of life in earthy ways not found in more sanitized places. Open food stalls are everywhere: a pervasive aroma of corn tortillas, roasting meats, chilies, and *garapiñados* (nuts cooked in caramelized sugar) are just a few of the pleasurable smells that mix with the noxious exhaust of too many vehicles or clogged drainage pipes. Air quality has been steadily improving over the past few years, however, and there are many days with clear blue skies.

Mexico City has a bit of an old-fashioned feel; it is comfortable with its long cultural heritage, not terribly concerned with trends or fads. Old style barbershops, wooden-door cantinas, dowdy ladies' corset shops, and glass-bottle pharmacies are found throughout the city, some of them untouched for 50 years or more. Modern Mexico City also has plenty of slick, high-rise stuff, and lots of super-rich people living behind walls, mostly in the western suburbs. Chic hotels, elegant restaurants and designer stores are here, but they tend to have the same global feeling as elsewhere. It's the energy of living tradition that makes this city distinctive.

You can feel a deep sense of ancient history here. The faces of many people, the food, and place names such as Chapultepec, Popocatepetl and Nezahualcoyotl reflect its pre-Hispanic past. A sense of the world not changing, and the embrace of history, give this city a special character, but with the forces of globalization pounding at the gates, I don't think it will last much longer. It's a good time to visit.

Mexico City is not for the faint-hearted traveler. The air is polluted, the traffic is beyond belief, it's in an earthquake zone, and not far from a smoking volcano. You don't come to relax or "get away from it all." You come to be seduced by a flourishing 700-year old culture, by people whose hearts are easily opened, and by the sheer audacity of it all. Keep your senses alert and you, the curious traveler, will be richly rewarded. I hope this book will enable you to discover Mexico City, and to love it as I do.

Travel Tips:
Planning, Arrival, Getting Around

BEFORE YOU GO:

Visit my blog: www.mexicocitydf.com

You'll find updates, articles, and new discoveries. I welcome your comments to keep the book as up-to-date and as useful as possible.

If you are reading this book in preparation for a move to Mexico City, be sure to check out my blog post entitled 'Moving to Mexico City': www.mexicocitydf.blogspot.mx/2008/10/moving-to-mexico-city.html

When to Visit: There is no bad time to visit Mexico City—the climate is as close to springtime year-round as you will find anywhere. My favorite month is March when the jacaranda trees are in full bloom—the huge clouds of lavender blossoms are a stunning sight. April and May can be hot but dry, December and January can be chilly at night, and the rainy season (late May through October) can bring some days of London-like gloom. But in general, Mexico City's climate is not extreme, and a week without sunshine is rare. The city is quiet between Christmas and New Year, but comes alive immediately afterwards for Día de los Tres Reyes Magos (January 6). Semana Santa (the week before Easter) is another quiet time, when anyone who can leaves town, making the city easier to get around. Día de Muertos (November 2) is a great time to travel anywhere in Mexico to experience one of its most moving traditions.

Documents: A passport is required to enter Mexico. Before leaving home, copy or scan your passport, credit cards, driver's license, and any other important documents. Send the scanned documents to yourself as an e-mail attachment. Keep them in a permanent file in your e-mail account for access anywhere in the world.

Learn some Spanish: While you can easily travel throughout Mexico without knowing the language—Mexicans are very helpful and accommodating—you will enhance your visit greatly with some elementary Spanish. Learn some basic greetings, numbers, words for ordering food, and you will be surprised at the way Mexicans open up to you. Even if you speak badly, they usually make you feel like an expert. If you are uncomfortable with Spanish, ask someone at your hotel to write out

Xochimilco

names and addresses of your destinations to show taxi drivers. The website www.studyspanish.com is useful.

ARRIVAL INFORMATION:

Airport: From the U.S. you cannot enter Mexico on a one-way ticket. You must prove how you plan to leave the country.

Mexico City has two terminals, connected by a monorail (for ticket holders only). Most, but not all, international flights use Terminal 2. Be sure to check your tickets for the correct terminal.

When you get to Passport Control you will be given a slip of paper — your tourist permit. Hold on to it as you will need it to leave the country. After claiming your luggage you must go through Customs (aduana in Spanish)—it is all clearly marked. At customs you will be asked to push a button which illuminates a red or green light at random. If you get the red light, your baggage will be searched, but in my experience this has been perfunctory. Through the doors in front of you is the Arrivals Area full of eager families and porters. Ask a porter to help you, even if you don't have much luggage—he can help guide you through the chaos. A 10 to 30 peso tip is normal—pay when you get to the taxi.

You must use pre-paid registered taxis to leave the airport—DO NOT go out on the street to hail a cab without a ticket. Buy your ticket (prices range from 100 to 300 pesos for a normal size taxi) at the counter outside the Arrivals Area, or go outside and get your ticket there. You will see the words "*Taxis Autorizados*" clearly marked, or ask your porter. Fares are determined by zones—just tell them where you are going. The cab driver will take the ticket and give you half as your receipt. Sometimes there is an additional charge if you have lots of luggage. Tipping is not customary, but always appreciated.

Money Saving Tip: If you arrive in Terminal 1, you can use a taxi stand (sitio) my neighbor Dolores, who works for the airlines, told me about that can save you up to 50%. Walking toward Sala A you'll see an overhead pedestrian bridge between Puertas 5 and 6. Take the escalator up and follow the sign for 'crew parking' and 'Aerotren'. The sitio is at the far end of the bridge, on the left, down the stairs. Metered taxis here cost about half of those mentioned above.

Metro: There is a metro stop at Terminal 1. The entrance is outside, past Sala A. Large suitcases or parcels are not permitted on the metro. Caution: if you are taking the metro to the airport, the station is called *Terminal Aerea* on the Yellow Line (#5)—do not get out at the stop marked *Aeropuerto*. I have yet to figure out the logic of this.

Metrobús: There is service to/from the airport to points in the Centro. In Terminal 1, it is located between Puertas 6 and 7. In Terminal 2, it's on the lower level, near Puerta 3. The fare is 30 pesos.

Bus: For bus travel beyond Mexico City, see the websites www.mexicoautobuses.com and www.ticketbus.com.mx which offers tickets online to many destinations. You can buy tickets for some bus lines at the MultiMarca ticket stand, Monte Piedad #11, between 5 de Mayo and Francisco I. Madero, across from the Zócalo and next door to McDonald's. Open daily 9 to 5. Cash only if you are a foreigner.

Money: ATMs (*cajeros automáticos*) are found all over the city for getting pesos. At the airport you'll see lots of money exchange places—

the rates are usually good here. Using your bankcard is more convenient than traveler's checks or cash, and the exchange rate is often better. The same is true of credit card purchases, although credit cards are not accepted at many smaller stores and restaurants. Be alert when you enter and leave ATM booths—there are accounts of robberies. Prices in Mexico are generally marked in pesos, but the $ is used before the number, confusing many Americans who think it means dollars. $50 means 50 pesos. It is unlikely that anyone in Mexico City will accept U.S. dollars or other foreign currency—except at a bank or fancy hotel.

CITY TRANSPORTATION

Car: I do not recommend renting a car for touring Mexico City unless you are familiar with the city or are a masochistic daredevil. Hiring a car and driver is relatively cheap here (from US$15/hour)—you can arrange it at most taxi sitios, or through your hotel.

Taxis: Taxis are everywhere in the city and fares are reasonable. Stories abound of taxi-related crime, but I've never had problems. My advice to first time visitors who do not speak Spanish is to use only *sitio* taxis (literally means "site" as they are found in specific locations marked by that word) which are registered and safe, or hotel taxis, which are more expensive but also reliable. Sitio locations are found in many of the more popular tourist destinations, or you can call them to pick you up anywhere in the city. If you find a cab driver you like, get his card so you can call him. Sitio cabs usually charge by zone, although some use meters in the daytime. Drivers often ask for a flat fee at night. It is very important to agree on a price beforehand if there is no meter. If a price seems exorbitant, it probably is. Most destinations within the center city should be under 200 pesos.

At taxi sitios through the city, you can arrange to pay by the hour (around US$15)—having a taxi driver meet you at your hotel is a great way to see the city without further transportation worries. It is not customary to tip taxi drivers (unless they provide an extra service such as waiting or carrying your bags), but it is always appreciated.

Expect to pay much more for Taxis de Turismo, which are found at hotels and some tourist sites, like the Museo de Antropología.

Here are a few sitio phone numbers:

Servi-Taxi	5271-2560
Radio-Taxi	5516-6020 or 5519-7690
Taxi-Mex	5538-0912
Sitio Parque México	5286-7129
Base Concord (airport)	5762-0756

If you do hail a cab on the street, take a few precautions. It is best to know where you are going and the mostly likely route by checking a map before you go. Every cab is required to have a visible license with a photo and a fare meter—don't enter cabs without these. Look for the letters A or B on the license plate or written on the side door. A statue of the Virgin of Guadalupe on the dashboard is another good sign.

Do not take any cab that solicits you—advice that holds true worldwide. Always use sitio taxis if you are travelling with luggage.

If you are leaving a restaurant or club at night, ask someone to call you a taxi. Many nightspots have taxis out front known to the management— make sure the doorman or other person in charge indicates the cab for you.

Carry a phone card with you to call taxis, or if you are here for a longer stay, you might consider buying a local cell phone, which can be purchased for as little as 350 pesos.

Uber: Smartphone users should take advantage of this excellent car service. Find details at www.uber.com

Traffic: Yes, the traffic is as bad as they say it is, but a few tips may help you from tearing your hair out. Try to avoid car/taxi travel during rush hours. *La quincena* is the term for the Friday closest to the first or the fifteenth of each month—payday for many people here. Everybody goes out to spend and have fun and the traffic is a nightmare—plan accordingly.

Buses, Peseros, Metrobús: There are thousands of bus lines in a Byzantine system. Small shelters on some corners indicate designated bus stops, but you can often get smaller buses to stop just by waving your hand. Prices vary—they are usually posted on the wall just over the

driver's head. If you don't see a fare sign, tell the driver your destination and he will tell you the amount, usually under 5 pesos, except the Metrobús, which is 6 pesos.

Bus routes are indicated by their final destinations, posted in the front window. I find two basic lines most helpful in getting around the city. Reforma is the major east-west thoroughfare—use buses here to get from the Centro Histórico to Parque Chapultepec and back. Look in the front window for Auditorio when going toward the park, and Hidalgo or Zócalo when heading toward the Centro.

Insurgentes, the city's longest street, runs north-to-south the entire length of the city and beyond. The Metrobús along Insurgentes has stops at most major intersections. These are larger buses with a designated lane, so it's often the fastest way south (Coyoacán and San Angel for example). A ride down Insurgentes presents a good view of the burgeoning Mexican middle class, with lots of glitzy shopping and eating places, and some interesting new high-rise office buildings. You must buy a rechargeable fare card before you board, sold from a machine at the entrance. **Check my blogpost** (http://mexicocitydf.blogspot.mx/2012/01/how-to-use-metrobus.html) for more details on getting a bus card. Be careful of the badly designed doors as they open and close!

Metro: The metro is fast, efficient, clean, cheap (5 pesos, less than 40 cents US), and the only metro in the world with real Aztec ruins (the Altar of Ehécatl, the Aztec god of wind, can be seen at the Pino Suárez station).

Different lines are both number and color coded, and each station is marked by a symbol. Trains are marked by their final destinations. Buy your ticket at the taquilla (ticket booth) and place it in the turnstile to enter. If you need to switch trains, follow the signs that say 'correspondencia'.

You will usually find metro maps on the wall near the taquilla, and maps by exit stairs showing aboveground street plans. Cars at either end of the metro tend to be less crowded. Front cars are reserved for women and children at peak hours. Avoid the metro during rush hours (7 to 10 am and 6 to 8 pm) unless you love massive crowds.

THE METRO

About 4 million people ride the metro every day, making it a great place for people watching.

Merchants and musicians pass through the cars, singing or selling their wares, altering their voices to curious high-pitched nasal sounds to sustain the vocal chords during long hours of work. A few vendors are children, at times disturbingly young, often unaccompanied by an adult. I once saw a young boy play the accordion while his sister passed the cup. Both of them were under 7 years old, but deep in their world-weary eyes they looked older than me. The norteña music he played was joyous and bouncy, creating an ironically upbeat soundtrack to a sadly poignant scene.

"Gente nice" (a mixed-idiom slang term for the well-dressed and well-bred) are rarely seen on the metro. Some of my Mexican friends, middle class and college-educated, have never been on the metro. As an ex-New Yorker, I'm used to riding a subway. I take the metro several times each week, often finding myself the tallest and whitest person in the car, but I have never felt uncomfortable.

Nothing bad has happened to me on the metro, but I stay alert, especially if it's crowded. Pay attention to your bags and pockets. Don't wear flashy jewelry. Keep cameras inside your bag, and keep bags and knapsacks in front of you. I never carry a wallet, just a photo ID, an ATM card, and enough cash for immediate needs—always in my front pocket. A Mexican woman friend rides the subway daily to work and never has problems. A tall blonde American friend who rode the subway alone became the object of unwanted sexual attention. I will leave it up to women traveling alone to judge for themselves.

Bicitaxis: Bicycle-taxi service is a delightful way to cover short distances in the Centro. Bicitaxis used to congregate around the Zócalo, but the city has been pushing them around, so they are a bit harder to find—you will notice them at major intersections in the Centro, especially in the area behind the Cathedral. Prices are determined by distance and weight—most rides within the Centro should be under US$5. You can also hire them by the hour (around 300 pesos/hour). Be sure to agree on the price before you start your ride.

Turibus: A good way to see a lot of the city without worrying about transportation is to take the Turibus (*www.turibus.com.mx)*, a red double-decker that passes by most of the major tourist attractions in the city. Headphones are available to hear commentary in several languages. Ask at your hotel for the stop nearest you, or check the website map.

Bicycle: The city's Ecobici program has become increasingly popular and now is available to visitors (*www.ecobici.df.gob.mx*). There are 275 stations scattered around town where you can pick up/drop off your bike. It took me a while to work up the courage to ride a bike here, but now I use one almost every day. I advise caution, as city drivers tend to be aggressive: don't expect courtesy, always be on the defensive. Sunday is a great day for bike riding along Reforma, which is closed to traffic from 9am to 2pm. On the last Sunday of each month a 32km route, free of all cars, loops around the city. Visitors can rent an Ecobici for one day (90 pesos), three days (180 pesos) or a week (300 pesos). You must go in person to the office (Nuevo León 78, between Michoacán and Laredo in Colonia Condesa, or Lafontaine near Masaryk in Polanco) with a passport and Visa or Mastercard. The office is open from 9 to 6 Monday–Friday and 10 to 2 Saturday.

Free Bikes are available at kiosks along Reforma, near the Cathedral, and several places in Polanco. Bikes must be returned to the same location. You must leave a credit card and passport. Here's the link to the map of station locations: *http://ciudadmexico.com.mx/mapas/cicloestaciones.htm*.

Pedestrian Alert: I have found some of the worst and rudest drivers in Mexico. Generally kind and considerate, Mexicans can turn into conquistadores behind the wheel of a car. Do not take for granted any right-of-way. Cross streets carefully—pedestrians are considered nuisances to be ignored or challenged. There is no driving test to obtain a license in Mexico—take that as a clue.

Bicitaxi

ADDITIONAL TIPS

Asking Directions: Mexicans do not like to say no, so they may give you directions even if they have no idea where you are going. I usually ask three people before I accept directions, unless someone seems extremely certain.

Planta Baja: The first floor of a building is called the planta baja, the next floor is 1, then 2, etc.—in elevators you will see PB, which is usually the lobby or entry level.

Business Hours: Most businesses, including markets, do not get rolling until 10am, so there's no need to hurry in the morning. Some smaller businesses close for comida (usually 2 to 4pm), but this is increasingly rare. Most museums and all of Parque Chapultepec are closed on Mondays.

Magazines: Published monthly, *Time Out* is available free at many shops and galleries, and has the best listings of all the magazines. You can find everything on their website *www.timeoutmexico.mx/df*

The weekly magazine *Tiempo Libre* lists movies, theater, music, dance, art exhibits, and more. It comes out every Thursday and is sold at most newsstands and at Sanborn's. *Chilango* magazine, published monthly, has listings of what's going on in the city as well, and if you read Spanish, there are some fun articles on city culture. (The word "chilango", formerly derogatory, is now a proud slang moniker for a Mexico City dweller.)

Maps: The app maps.me is an excellent resource. Guia Roji makes the best maps as well as a detailed book of all city streets, indispensable if you live here. It's available at Sanborns, and online at www.guiaroji.com.mx;

Government-run tourist kiosks located in the Zócalo, and in Parque Chapultepec are a good source for very good, free city maps.

Telephone: Landline telephones within Mexico City have 8 digits. Cell phones numbers in the city begin with 044-55, (when dialed from a land line) followed by 8 digits. If calling cell to cell, the 044 is not necessary.

When calling a Mexico City number from the U.S. or Canada dial 011-52-55 before the 8-digit number. If calling a Mexico City number from another part of Mexico, dial 01-55 before the 8 numbers. To call the U.S. from Mexico dial 001 before the area code and number.

Most pay phones work with a card, which can be purchased at newsstands, pharmacies, OXXO, and 7-11 stores, and those displaying a LADATEL sign. It's a good idea to have one for calling taxis or possible emergencies—telephones that accept coins are hard to find these days.

Dress: Mexicans are fairly casual in their dress, but always neat and clean, and relatively modest. At concerts or fancy restaurants you will see everything from tuxedos to t-shirts. Few Mexican men wear shorts in the city. Short-shorts on women might be miscontrued.

Smoking: It is not permitted to smoke in most public venues in the city, but many restaurants have tables outdoors for those who wish to indulge.

A FEW IMPORTANT NUMBERS:

Dial 066 for Emergencies.

Dial 040 for Directory Assistance.

Dial 5658-1111 for Locatel, a service that helps you locate anything, even if you don't have an exact name or address—very useful, but only in Spanish.

SOME USEFUL WEBSITES:

www.conaculta.gob.mx: Cultural events, click on English version

www.ticketmaster.com.mx: To buy tickets for cultural events

www.ciudadmexico.com.mx: Good transport maps

www.festival.org.mx: Festival de Centro Histórico in early spring

www.guiadelcentrohistorico.mx: Guide to Centro Histórico

¡Aguas! (Literally = waters) means "watch out!" in Mexico. This warning dates from colonial times when, lacking a sewer system, dirty water would be thrown out of windows. If you hear it, look around. *¡Ojo!* is an alternative.

Heads & Feet: Many Mexicans are short and the city is built to accommodate them. Watch your head!—especially in market areas, where sharp metal awnings appear unexpectedly. Watch your feet! Holes, cracks, and bumps in the pavement are frequent.

Altitude: Mexico City is about 7000 feet above sea level. Combined with polluted air, the altitude can affect some travelers. You might notice shortness of breath or tiring easily at first, but this usually passes in a day or two. Be careful with alcohol, especially when you first arrive: at this altitude it packs more of a wallop.

Health Concerns: Stories of "Montezuma's revenge" and other intestinal problems are not uncommon, but if you follow a few basic guidelines (see "Street Food" section) you should be OK. If you have diarrhea for more than two days, or if it is accompanied by fever, call a doctor. Dehydration can be a serious problem associated with diarrhea —drink some Pedialyte, available at pharmacies, to restore electrolytes. Do not eat fruits or vegetables unless they have been peeled or disinfected. You can assume that any restaurant mentioned in this book will be serving safe, clean produce, ice and salads.

Water: Don't drink tap water in Mexico! I know an American who lived here for a year and only drank tap water, seemingly without problems, but don't take a chance. If you want to reduce your consumption of small plastic bottles, and avoid putting more money in the pockets of the Coca Cola company, which bottles most of the water here, ask for *agua de garafón* in restaurants. It's purified water from larger plastic containers: Mexico City law now requires that all restaurants offer this water for free.

Safety: If you follow common-sense rules of city behavior, you should be fine. Every visitor I have known has been positively impressed with how safe and inviting the city feels. Be sure to read and understand the above section on taxis.

Bathrooms: Things are much better than they used to be, but bathroom hygiene in Mexico is often not up to expected standards. The words *sanitario, servicios* or '*WC*' are used for public bathrooms , but 'baños' will work if you're looking for one. Some bathrooms in public places have attendants. Americans can be baffled by this custom, as such jobs don't exist in the first world. Keep in mind that most attendants work just for tips.

In markets, gas stations and some public places there is a charge of a few pesos to use the facilities. Be aware that toilet paper is often handed out near the entrance and is usually not found inside the stalls.

Finding a bathroom while you are out and about: The Sanborn's chain can always be counted on for clean bathrooms. Hotels and department stores are also a good bet. I have made note of some of these in the Walking Tours.

Tipping and Bargaining: Leave waiters 10 to 15% in restaurants. If you're paying by credit card, you may be asked if you want to "*cerrar la cuenta*", which means adding the tip—just say the percentage you care to leave. Taxi drivers do not expect tips, but it is always appreciated. Gas station attendants are tipped—a few pesos will do. Some foreigners think that you must bargain for everything in Mexico, or pay in US dollars to get a better price. These are largely outdated concepts unless you are buying in quantity, or contracting a service such as a car

Chapultepec Park

and driver. Bargaining in most places will just make you look silly and cheap. Many travelers ask if they have paid too much for something. My advice is if you are comfortable paying the price, then the price is right. Travel with a sense of generosity in your heart and you will have a better time.

Panhandlers: Awareness of poverty in Mexico is never far from one's eyes, and while it is rarely oppressive, we are often asked to help the needy. Everyone must figure out his or her own strategy—mine is to give to the elderly and anyone who makes music, even if they play badly.

Tranquility Breaks: The city can easily overwhelm the traveler with its intensity, so plan some restful breaks into your day. Churches are always good for relative
quiet anywhere in the city. Take a walking tour of Colonia Roma or Condesa (especially tranquil on Sundays and holidays), or Coyoacán (better on weekdays), or walk through Parque Chapultepec (peaceful only during the week),
or stop in a café.

Qi (*317 Amsterdam, Col. Condesa, www.centroqi.mx*) is an upscale gym; their spa is open to the public and offers great massages.

Travel Beyond Mexico City

Located in the geographical center of the country, Mexico City is the perfect jumping off point for many excursions, and there are bus or plane connections to just about anywhere. Here are a few of my favorite places.

HEADING SOUTH AND EAST, the colonial cities of **Puebla** and **Oaxaca** can be combined in one trip. Puebla is about 2 hours away by car or bus, Oaxaca another 4 hours. There's an airport in Oaxaca.

A 3 to 4 hour drive from Puebla, **Cuetzalan del Progreso** is a magical town with a great weekend market. If you're looking for 'old Mexico', you'll find it here.

Jalapa, about 2 hours from Puebla, has one of the finest pre-Hispanic art museums in the country.

NORTH OF MEXICO CITY, the towns of **Querétaro**, **San Miguel de Allende** and **Guanajuato** can easily be combined into one trip by bus (ETN or Primera Plus bus lines from Terminal Norte) or car, spending a few days in each place. The latter two have sizeable ex-pat communities; both would be good choices to rent a house and just hang out for a while.

Malinalco is a '*Pueblo Mágico*', two hours southwest of Mexico City. It has a small Aztec ruin, lots of churches, and a traditional street market. It's a lovely place for a low-key travel experience. It can be reached by Aguila bus lines from Observatorio station: take one of the frequent buses to Chalma, from there a ten minute taxi to Malinalco.

HEADING WEST to the state of **Michoacán**, the towns of **Morelia**, **Pátzcuaro** and **Uruapan** could easily fill a week or more of travel time. Heading further west to **Guadalajara**, you could fly back to Mexico City.

There are two beach resorts within driving distance of Mexico City. **Acapulco**, whose old town is a bit run down, with the exception of the fabulously restored '50's Hotel Boca Chica. **Pie de la Cuesta**, 20 minutes from central Acapulco, is a virgin beach dotted with a few small hotels and is a good destination for those on a budget. **Zihuatanejo** still retains some of its old fishing village charm while Ixtapa, next door is like a glossy shopping mall, though it has an airport.

Malinalco

Puerto Escondido, on the coast of Oaxaca state, is probably the best fly-to destination for a beach vacation. It is a long, twisting drive from Oaxaca City.

BUDGET AIRLINES IN MEXICO: Three airlines offer inexpensive flights within Mexico, and some to points within the U.S. Be sure to check their baggage claim policies, which can add to the cost of your ticket.

Viva Aerobus: www.vivaaerobus.com

Interjet: www.interjet.com.mx

Volaris: www.volaris.com

Register your email address on the website to receive updates about special offers. You can also "like" their Facebook pages, then point the cursor over the word like, click 'Get Notifications' and 'Show in News Feed'. Some offers may appear on Facebook only.

Palacio de Bellas Artes

Where to Sleep

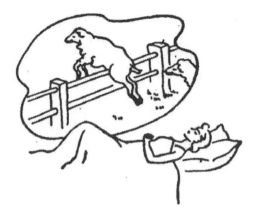

The Centro Histórico is a great location for first-time visitors. It is the heart of Mexico City where you can really feel its 700-year history. There are Aztec temples, bustling street energy, majestic colonial buildings, and great museums—all within a walkable area.

If the Centro's frenzy is too much for you, the best options are Colonias Condesa and Roma, both older residential neighborhoods with lively restaurants and cafes, tree-lined streets and a few small parks. Polanco is an upscale neighborhood with lots of high-end hotels and restaurants—a bit blander than Condesa or Roma, but more comfortable if the rough edges of Mexico City bother you. Zona Rosa is another popular and conveniently located hotel area, but you might end up feeling like you're staying in a big shopping mall.

If you're here for more than a few days, you might consider dividing your time between the Centro and one of the quieter areas to get a better overall view of the city.

Renting an apartment in Mexico City is a great option.

Often cheaper than hotels, the websites **www.airbnb.com** and **www.vrbo.com** both have good listings.

Hostels

If you are travelling alone, or if you want to meet other travelers, hostels can be a good choice. But for two people, it is usually not a bargain, as you can easily find a private hotel room for the same price or less.

Downtown Beds (Isabel la Católica 30, Centro, www.downtownbeds. com) is the hippest hostel in town and offers access to their rooftop pool.

Hostal Centro Histórico Regina (5 de Febrero 53, Centro, www.hostalcentrohistoricoregina.com) is in a colonial building on a pedestrian street, with a rooftop party terrace.

Hostel Mundo Joven Catedral (República de Guatemala 8, Centro, www.mundojovenhostels.com) This popular hostel boasts a great location overlooking the Zócalo.

Hostal Virreyes (Izazága 8, Centro, tel. 5521-4180, www.hostalvirreyes.com.mx) If you are planning a long stay, they have cheap monthly rates—attracts a hip, young crowd.

The website www.bedandbreakfastworld.com lists small b&bs.

Hotels

In each section below listings are from least to most expensive.

CENTRO HISTÓRICO

For the traveler on a budget there are several options near the Zócalo, especially along Cinco de Mayo, with rooms for around US$30. These places are usually pretty basic, but perfectly clean, with private bathrooms. Rooms tend to vary—some have no exterior windows— so ask to see one first. Here are few to choose from:

Hotel Juárez (Cda. de Cinco de Mayo 17, tel. 5512-6929)

Hotel Rioja (Cinco de Mayo 45, tel. 5521-8333)

Hotel Washington (Cinco de Mayo 54, tel. 5512-3502)

Avoid the nearby hotels Zamora, which is a bit dingy, and the Canada, which is overpriced.

Hotel Isabel (*Isabel la Católica 63, tel. 5518-1213, www.hotel-isabel. com*), a few blocks from the Zócalo, is a budget option that has long been a popular bohemian hangout.

Hotel Gillow (*Isabel la Católica 17 at the corner of Cinco de Mayo, tel. 5512-2078, www.hotelgillow.com*) At around US$60 for a double, this place is a good deal. The best rooms on the 6th floor have terraces —there is an especially nice single room (#601) with a small terrace adjoining a church bell tower. They don't take reservations for the terrace rooms, however, so ask when you check in.

Hotel Catedral (*Donceles 95, tel. 5518-5232, www.hotelcatedral.com*) Owned by the same company, and in the same price range as the Hotel Gillow, this is the choice of several friends when they visit the city. There is a funny little terrace on the 6th floor with a view of the Cathedral where you can order food or drinks to be sent up.

Hotel Majestic (*on the Zócalo at Madero, tel. 5521-8600, www.hotelmajestic.com*) This hotel has a lovely colonial style lobby and rooms starting at about US$130. The rooftop terrace is a great place for breakfast or a drink.

NH Centro Histórico (*Palma 42, tel. 5130-1850, www.nh-hotels.com*) This sleek hotel is a few blocks from the Zócalo. There is a good view from the restaurant.

Hilton Mexico City Reforma (*Avenida Juárez, facing the Alameda, tel. 5130-5300, www3.hilton.com*) is a modern high-rise affair, glamorous, if a bit cold. It does have that big hotel buzz about it, and all the amenities you expect.

Gran Hotel de la Ciudad de Mexico (*on the Zócalo, entrance on 16 de Septiembre, tel. 1083-7700, www.granhotelciudaddemexico.com.mx*) This art nouveau masterpiece from 1899, with an impressive stained glass ceiling over the lobby, has been remodeled in standard fancy hotel style. The rooftop terrace has a great view of the Zócalo.

Downtown (*Isabel la Católica 30, tel. 5282-2199, www.downtown-mexico.com*) Trendy and fabulous, this hotel has both high-end rooms and dormitory beds, and a rooftop terrace with pool.

COLONIA CONDESA

Hotel Roosevelt (*Insurgentes Sur 287, corner of Yucatan, tel. 5208-6813, www.hotelroosevelt.com.mx*) is the least expensive option in Colonia Condesa. It has ugly art on the walls, but it's clean and comfortable and conveniently located for exploring Condesa and Roma—many of our friends stay here. Inside rooms are quieter.

The Red Tree House (*Culiacan 6, Condesa, tel. 5584-3829, www.theredtreehouse.com*) This small B&B, in a remodeled old house, is located on a quiet residential street in Condesa. Book way ahead—it's very popular.

Condesa Haus (*Cuernavaca 142, tel. 5256-2429, www.condesahaus.com*) This converted old house on a quiet street is near Condesa's night life.

Condesa DF (*Avenida Veracruz 102, tel. 5241-2600, www.condesadf.com*) This small, trendy hotel, with its hip decor, is where many celebrities stay. The restaurant and rooftop bar are hot spots on weekends, so ask about noise.

Colonia Condesa

COLONIA ROMA

Hotel Milan (*Alvaro Obregón 94, 5584-0222, www.hotelmilan.com. mx*) The Milan has the best location in Roma, directly across from Casa Lamm. The renovated rooms are compact but pleasant, and a good deal.

Four Points by Sheraton (*Álvaro Obregón 38, 1085-9510, www.fourpoints.com/coloniaroma*) This renovated high-rise, a few blocks from the Milan, is a more upscale choice. The expensive rooms have giant tubs in the room, but are no nicer otherwise.

La Casona (*Durango 280, tel. 52863001, www.mexicoboutiquehotels. com/lacasona*) Located in Colonia Roma Norte, but within walking distance of Condesa, this remodeled mansion offers comfort and old-style charm. Check online for special offers.

Colonia Roma

OTHER LOCATIONS AROUND TOWN

El Patio 77 (*Izcazbalceta 77, San Rafael, 5592-8452, www.elpatio77. com*) The city's first eco-friendly hotel is a charmingly re-done old home in a funky, but interesting, neighborhood.

Hotel Maria Cristina (*Rio Lerma 31, Colonia Juárez, tel. 5703-1787, www.hotelmariacristina.com.mx*) A colonial style hotel in a quiet residential neighborhood north of the Zona Rosa, once popular with the artsy set. The lobby has charm and the rooms are clean and efficient, if not exactly high style.

Roommate Valentina (*Amberes 27, tel. 5080-4500, www.valentina. room-matehotels.com*) Hip, cool, and right in the middle of the Zona Rosa.

Camino Real Mexico (*Mariano Escobedo 700, Colonia Anzures, tel. 5263-8888, www.caminoreal.com/mexico*) Located near the entrance of Parque Chapultepec near Polanco, this impressive hotel was designed by Ricardo Legorreta, one of Mexico's leading architects, who was inspired by the vast spaces of Teotihuacán. It has a fun big-hotel feel with flashy restaurants and bars. Rooms vary, so check several.

Las Alcobas (*Masaryk 390, Polanco, tel. 3300-3900, www.lasalcobas. com*) This boutique hotel is the top choice for location and comfort in Polanco. It's restaurant, Anatol, is one of the city's best

W Hotel (*Campos Elíseos 252, Polanco, tel. 9138-1800, www.star-woodhotels.com*) If you want to stay in the most "fabulous" place in town, this is it. Here you will find high-end design and glamorous people.

Food:
What and Where to Eat

Mexico's culinary history dates back to pre-conquest times and includes influences from Spanish, French and Lebanese immigrants, among others. Corn, tomatoes, chilies, avocados, beans, turkey, chocolate and vanilla were first encountered in the New World, and they remain fundamental to Mexican cooking.

If you know Mexican food from having eaten it in other countries, you'll likely be in for a pleasant surprise in the capitol: it's a world-class food town. The quality of fruits, vegetables, meat and fish is high. Plastic-wrapped, pre-cooked or highly processed food is not the norm here, so basic ingredients have real flavor. Contrary to common wisdom, most Mexican dishes are not particularly spicy, although salsa is always available to turn up the heat.

☛ **For a more complete guide to eating out in the city I recommend:** *Good Food in Mexico City: Food Stalls, Fondas, and Fine Dining* by Nicholas Gilman. His blog is another great source of information: www.goodfoodmexicocity.com

The following is a brief list of some of the most common and popular foods you will encounter.

Aguas Frescas: Literally "fresh waters", these are traditional drinks made with fresh fruits and vegetables (among other ingredients), then pureed in a blender with sugar and water. They are found in most Mexican restaurants and food stalls, although sometimes you won't see them on the menu, so be sure to ask. The most common flavors are jamaica (hibiscus flower), tamarindo (pulp from tamarind seeds) and horchata (made from rice, sometimes almonds—there is no milk in this white drink) as well as a host of fruits: mango, guava, papaya, watermelon and cantaloupe are favorites. NOTE: plain purified drinking water is called agua natural--if you just ask for 'agua' in some places you might be served agua fresca. If you want purified water not in a bottle, ask for agua de garrafón in restaurants. By law, all Mexico City restaurants must offer free purified drinking water.

Mercado Jamiaca

Antojitos: This is a food category, not a dish, but you will see the word a lot. Its meaning (literally "before the eyes") can vary, but it most often refers to corn-based appetizers, anything made with tortillas or *masa de maíz* (corn dough). They are eaten as a light meal or snack (although they can often be quite filling). Like Italian pasta, a basic ingredient, corn, appears in a variety of shapes and sizes, and affects the taste accordingly. Some of the most common antojitos are tacos, quesadillas, tlacoyos, gorditas, sopes, panuchos, tamales, huaraches, and enchiladas.

Chiles en nogada: This classic Mexican dish is popular around Fiestas Patrias (Independence Day, 15th of September), but is served year-round in some restaurants. Green poblano chilies are filled with a mixture of chopped pork and raisins or other dried fruit, topped with a creamy, slightly sweet sauce made of ground walnuts, then sprinkled with red pomegranate seeds. The three colors represent the Mexican flag. This dish is usually served at room temperature.

Chocolate: The Aztecs, who mixed cocoa with chili and drank it for festive occasions, introduced it to the rest of the world. Today, the best way to try Mexican chocolate is mixed with hot milk and served with churros, a sweet fried dough stick. Churros y Chocolate 'El Moro' (Eje Central 42 near Uruguay, Centro) has been around since 1935 and is open 24 hour a day. Hexagonal boxes of Abuela or Ibarra brands of chocolate, available at any grocery store, make nice gifts (break up the tablets of chocolate and mix in a blender with hot milk). Chocolate candy and desserts, on the other hand, are often disappointing, even though they might look great. I love chocolate and have eaten many mediocre chocolate desserts in search of the truly delicious. Sanborn's, that chain of restaurant/stores that always seems to come in handy, sells chocolates by weight—100 grams is a good amount to start with. Of the many choices a few are really good. I recommend *maronet amargo*, avellaneda, *hojas de cassis, tortugas*, and the *almendras*.

Comida Corrida: You will see these words all over town in *fondas* and *comedores*, simple eateries that cater to working class Mexicans looking for an economic home-cooked meal. The word corrida refers to the 'running' sequence of courses. A complete meal, consisting of soup, rice, main course and often dessert and beverage, can be had for under five dollars. Sometimes the food is bland and watery, but you can also find hearty and delicious meals. Look for places that are clean and busy.

Frutas: Fresh, ripe fruit is easy to come by; you will probably see papaya and *melón* (cantaloupe) on most breakfast menus. *Plátanos* (bananas) are exceptionally flavorful in Mexico. The very little ones,

called *dominicos*, are my favorite. You may notice *zapotes negros* in the market: about the size of an orange with thin green skin and black flesh, they are sold very ripe and look like they are about to fall apart. It is sometimes served as a dessert, pureed with orange juice and tequila, or as an ice cream flavor. You'll see mangos sold on sticks with chili and lime by street vendors. The familiar big magenta mangos sold for export are the least tasty, and more likely to be stringy. The smaller, lime-green ones (sometimes called *manilas*) are best. *Pitahayas* can be seen in paintings by Frida Kahlo, who was drawn to their exotic appearance. They look like small hot-pink footballs with tiny fins, with a bluish flesh flecked with tiny black seeds. The flavor is similar to kiwi, but milder. Red and green tunas are cactus fruits best enjoyed as a drink (they have lots of tiny black seeds that need to be strained). Ping-pong ball sized yellow guayabas are fragrant fruits also best in drinks because of their seeds—try a *licuado* of plátano and guayaba.

Gorditas: "Little fat ones" are pockets of corn masa, cooked on a griddle and stuffed with beans, meat, nopales, etc. This is one of the most common street foods in Mexico City.

Guacamole: Most visitors to Mexico will know this avocado concoction, which has many variations, but be sure to try it here and find out what great avocados taste like.

Jugos: You will notice fresh fruit juices at street stalls throughout the city, lined up in a colorful display. Orange, carrot, and beet are the most common. Try a vampiro which includes all three, and sometimes celery, too. (Do not drink pure beet juice—it wreaks havoc on your stomach.) Jugos Canadá (see Walking Tour of Centro Histórico #1) is a great place to go for all kinds of juices.

Limonada: Lemonade is available everywhere in Mexico and is delicious and refreshing. Made with small green limes called limones, it is mixed with either plain water (agua natural) or sparkling water (agua mineral).

Mezcal: Has become very fashionable in Mexico City over the past few years—it's often served at art openings. It is a variation of tequila, made from different types of agave. Although produced all over the country, much of it comes from the state of Oaxaca. It usually has a smoky, almost charcoal-like, taste.

Mole: *(pronounced MO-lay)* is a thick, complex sauce of chilies, spices and nuts or seeds, and sometimes chocolate. There are as many variations as there are cooks. The term "más mexicano que mole" is like saying "as American as apple pie". It is considered by many to be the national dish. Mole poblano was supposedly invented by the nuns of a Puebla convent who wanted to impress a visiting bishop by creating a new sauce that combined ingredients from both Europe and Mexico. The moles most frequently found in Mexico City are *rojo* or *poblano* (which really looks dark brown), *negro* (from Oaxaca) and *verde*, which has no chocolate and is thickened with pumpkin seeds. Mole is often served with a piece of chicken, turkey, pork or as enchiladas (sometimes called enmoladas). My all-time favorite mole is served in Fonda Mi Lupita, a hole-in-the-wall in the Centro (see p. 45.)

Nopales: Cactus paddles are eaten as a vegetable throughout Mexico. You will see them at most taco and tlacoyo stands, as a topping. *Ensalada de nopales* (cactus salad with onions, cilantro, and tomato) is a good way to try them; it's available in most traditional Mexican restaurants. Nopales have a mild, slightly acidic, green bean-like flavor, and, if not cooked properly, can be slimy like okra.

Postres: Mexico, though not famous for its desserts, offers a few classics I recommend. *Flan* (egg custard) is served everywhere (avoid the bright yellow, rubbery kind which is made from mix). *Pastel de Tres Leches* is a rich layer cake made with whole milk, evaporated milk and sweetened condensed milk. *Pay de limón* (lemon pie) and *pay de nuez* (pecan pie) are favorites you will find on many menus. *Chongos* are odd-looking curds of sweet milk in sugar syrup that aren't attractive to look at but become addictive. Mexican bakeries (pastelerias) offer lots of tempting cakes and cookies. Although the variety of shapes, sizes and colors is impressive, you will find that most of them taste pretty much the same.

Pozole: This hearty, satisfying soup, almost a stew, has many regional variations. Red pozole, the most common, has a pork and tomato base, contains large corn kernels (hominy), and is served with radish, lettuce, onion and oregano which added according to taste. Less common are *pozole blanco* (without tomato) and pozole verde which uses ground pumpkin seeds as the thickener.

Pulque: This viscous lightly alcoholic drink was used in Aztec rituals and has a long association as a drink of the common man, but like mezcal it has become trendy recently. It is made by fermenting the sap of the maguey or agave plant. It has a thick texture and a yeasty taste. *Curados* are pulques that have been flavored with fruits, vegetables or nuts. It is usually served in pulquerias and occasionally in restuarants specializing in regional food.

Quesadillas: Are often prepared along with tlacoyos at street stalls. Most commonly, a large corn tortilla is filled, folded and cooked on a comal. There are many kinds of fillings; my favorites are *flor de calabaza* (squash blossom flowers), *huitlacoche* (corn fungus with a mushroom-like taste), and *quelites* (any wild, spinach-like green).

Sopa: You can always count on good, homemade soup in Mexican restaurants. *Caldo de gallina* is chicken soup like grandma used to make—order this if your stomach needs a rest. My favorite soups are sopa de tortilla or sopa azteca, made with chicken broth, tomatoes, chilies, fried tortilla strips, avocado and cheese. *Sopa de flor de calabaza,* made with squash blossoms, and *sopa de ajo*, garlic soup presented with an egg floating in it, are also traditional favorites.

Sope: An open disk of corn masa, its edges pinched up to form a side, is fried and then topped with beans, chicken, chorizo; the variety is endless. These are often served as appetizers in restaurants or at street stalls. (Don't confuse sope with sopa, which is soup.)

Tacos: A taco here is a soft corn tortilla with a small amount of filling, rolled up and eaten with your hands. The crispy shells with ground beef, yellow cheese and lettuce that are sold as tacos in the U.S. are not found in Mexico City. When a wheat tortilla is used, it is called a burrito, more common in the north. Tacos are found everywhere, eaten day and night, and they can be considered essential to most Mexican diets. Meat is the preferred filling, but vegetable and seafood can be found. Most popular are *carnita*s (chopped roast pork), *barbacoa* (pit-cooked sheep or goat), *chicharrón* (pork rind), but you can also find tacos made of eyes, ears, nose and brain. A food icon of Mexico City is the *taco al pastor*, which reflects Arab influence in Mexican cuisine: small slices of seasoned pork are cut from a rotating spindle (you will notice them all over town) and served with a bit of pineapple, chopped onion, cilantro and salsa.

THE BEST TACO JOINTS IN TOWN

Salón Corona *(Bolivar 24, Centro)*
This belly-up-to-the-bar kind of place, offering beer on
tap, has been feeding happy taco eaters since 1928.
The *bacalao* (dried salt cod) and mole verde are highly
recommended.

El Huequito *(Ayuntamiento 21, corner López, Centro)*
This tiny operation – "huequito" means hole-in-the-wall -
has been in its niche since 1959, and was probably one
of the first places in the city to serve al pastor. It won
Chowzter.com's award as best taco in the world!

El Tizoncito *(Tamaulipas 122 near Nuevo León; several other
branches around town)* They claim to be the originator of
tacos al Pastor - quien sabe? But they are just about the
best and their salsas are too.

Tacos El Güero
*(Av. Amsterdam 135
near Michoacán,
Condesa)* These are
my favorite *tacos de
guisado*, with several
vegetarian choices:
try the cooked leafy
greens *quelites* or
acelgas (swiss chard)
or *coliflór* (fried cauliflower.)

El Pescadito *(Atlixco 38, corner Juan Escutia, Condesa)*
Tacos of Baja style fried fish and shrimp as well as the
tuna-like marlin.

Tacos Alvaro O *(Alvaro Obregón 90 near Orizaba,
open 1 - 11p.m.)* This popular corner spot serves classic
grilled meat tacos

A good taquería will have an alluring selection of salsas to spice things up. The other major category is *tacos de guisados,* cooked or stewed fillings, sometimes including vegetarian options.

Tamales: Don't leave Mexico without eating a *tamal* (singular form of the word in Spanish), even if you think you know them from other places. Tamales vary from region to region, but the basic idea is ground corn, wrapped in its husk and steamed. The masa (corn dough) is mixed with lard and usually contains a small amount of filling: chicken or pork or cheese with red or green sauce, mole, or strips of chile poblano are the most common.

Tamales Oaxaqueños are wrapped in banana leaves and have a smoother texture. The filling is really only a flavoring; the main event is the corn itself, its flavor and texture. Tamales are usually eaten in the morning and at night. In residential zones, market areas, outside metro stations, you will see vendors tending large shiny steel containers with steam escaping from the edge.

The best tamales I've eaten have always been from street vendors, but you can find them in some restaurants, too, especially on breakfast menus. Each year around Candelaria (February 2) there is a *Festival de Tamales* at the cultural center of Coyoacán that is worth the trip: tamales from all over Latin America are sold. Along with tamales, Mexicans often drink *atole*, a thick, hot drink made of finely ground corn, sometimes rice, and usually flavored with fruit (guayaba is a favorite), chocolate, vanilla or even coffee. I am not a big fan of the drink—for me it is too rich to have with tamales—but it can be very comforting on a cold winter morning.

Tequila: Mexico's most famous alcoholic drink is made from the heart of the agave plant. Many foreigners only drink it mixed as a margarita, but few Mexicans order it that way. If you want to appear more like a native, order 'un tequila' (not "una" - the word is masculine) with *sangrita* (literally "little blood"). You will be served two small glasses; one with straight tequila and one with a spicy red drink made of tomato juice with various additions, usually pomegranate or orange juice and hot sauce. Alternate sips from the two glasses. There are three basic types of tequila: *blanco, reposado,* and *añejo.* Reposados are aged and usually amber colored (and tend to be more expensive), but some people prefer the stronger bite of the clear blancos—it is purely a matter of personal taste. Añejos have been aged longer and tend to be smoother. Most bars have good selections, which waiters can explain, but be sure to ask prices as some get very expensive, especially if the waiter seems to be pushing his choice.

Mezcal: Also very popular, is made by a slightly different process and has a smoky flavor. Tequila is really a form of mezcal; its original name was "mezcal de Tequila".

Tlacoyos: These eye-shaped corn antojitos are found on street corners and near markets throughout the city. Almost always made by women with a comal (a round metal or clay plate atop a charcoal burner), they were probably eaten by the Aztecs in much the same form.

Corn masa is shaped by hand into a flat lozenge and filled with beans or cheese (my top choice is habas—fava beans), then cooked on a dry griddle. When done, it's topped with chopped nopales (cactus), onions, cilantro, grated cheese and red or green salsa.

Tortas: Mexico's version of the sandwich, supposedly invented by an Italian immigrant as a variation of paninni, is a soft roll (bolillo) stuffed with a wide range of ingredients. Popular choices are *milanesa* (pounded and fried meat), *pierna* (roast pork), and *choriqueso* (cheese and sausage). Garnishes include tomato, onion, avocado, cheese, lettuce and, of course, chile jalapeño or chipotle.

Tortillas: The staff of life of Mexican cuisine, the ubiquitous tortilla is essentially ground corn flattened into a 4 to 6" disc and cooked on a dry griddle (tortillas are sometimes made of wheat, more common in the north). Millions are eaten daily—and have been for centuries. They are the basic ingredient for tacos, enchiladas, tostadas, burritos, chilaquiles, flautas, and a host of other Mexican dishes. Fried tortilla chips, served as a snack or appetizer, are called *totopos*.

MEAL TIMES IN MEXICO

Desayuno *(Breakfast)* A morning meal can be served any time up until comida. The word almuerzo is sometimes used for a late morning meal, like brunch. Tamales and atole, eaten at street stands, is a common breakfast combo for many in the city.

Comida *(Lunch)* This is the main meal of the day for most Mexicans and is usually not eaten before 2 pm It's hard to find a place, except for big chain restaurants, open for lunch before 1pm. Mexicans love to sobremesar, sit around and chat after eating, so meals can last many hours. The American idea of eating, paying and leaving seems strange to Mexicans, and it is considered rude to be handed the check without asking for it.

Cena *(Dinner)* The evening meal is usually a simple affair in most Mexican homes, but going out for dinner is becoming more a part of Mexico City nightlife. Mexicans rarely go out for dinner before 8 p.m., often much later. A number of restaurants, particularly those specializing in seafood, are only open for comida, so be sure to check.

Sundays, many city restaurants, especially upscale ones, only open for comida and close at 6, or are closed entirely; be sure to check.

Where to Eat

(If telephone numbers are given, reservations are recommended)
$: under 150 pesos pp, $$: 150-300, $$$: over 300

CENTRO HISTÓRICO

El Cardenal *(Palma 23 and Juárez 70, inside the Hotel Hilton,
www.elcardenal.com.mx)* Traditional but modern Mexican cuisine; the
Palmas location has more charm, the Hilton is more glamorous. I love
the sopa seca de elote here, an upscale variation of esquites, a popular
street food. $$

Sanborns Palacio de los Azulejos *(Entrance at Cinco de Mayo or
Madero, near Eje central, open 24 hours)* The restaurant opened by the
American Sanborn brothers at the turn of a century has become a chain,
but the original, set in a pretty 18th century patio is still an obligatory
stop for all visitors. Best for breakfast. $

Café de Tacuba *(Calle Tacuba 28, www.cafedetacuba.com.mx)* This
landmark institution (founded in 1912) offers a veritable dictionary of
classic Mexican dishes (enchiladas, sopes, chalupas, chiles rellenos) in
a beautiful colonial- style interior. Strolling musicians add to the festive
atmosphere. $$

Café El Popular *(Cinco de Mayo 50)* Open around the clock, this
simple, homey place has been run by the same Chinese/Mexican family
for 65 years. The reasonably priced food is classic Mexican. $

Café del Palacio *(Lobby of the Palacio de Bellas Artes)* This pretty
restaurant is good for a light lunch, or pre-concert snack. $$

Limosneros *(Allende 3, near Tacuba, Tel 5521 5576)* This stylish
restaurant and bar, set in a restored colonial building, does creative
Mexican cooking and serves well chosen artisanal mezcals and beers.
It's a good place for a romantic date and is open late. $$$

Restaurante San Francisco *(San Ildefonso 40, Monday - Saturday,
lunch only)* Set in a colonial building, this popular place offers food of
Tlaxcala, with an inexpensive comida corrida.$

Café el Mayor *(República de Argentina 17)* The view of the Templo

Mayor may astonish you more than the food here, but it is lovely. $

Puro Corazón *(Monte Piedad 11, 8 am - 9 pm)* Go here for the best Zócalo views and gussied up Mexican classic dishes. $$

Fonda Mi Lupita *(Buen Tono 22, open daily 1-6, lunch only)* This humble place specializes in just about the best mole in the world. $

Coox Hanal *(Isabel la Católica 83, near Mesones, brunch and lunch only)* My favorite Yucatecan restuarant offers such classics as spicy red *cochinita pibil, panuchos, papadzules* and *pan de cazón.* $

Restaurante Al Andalus *(Mesones 171, Centro, daily 9 am - 6 pm)* This is one of the best Middle Eastern places in the city, located in a very commercial area near La Merced; it's set in a pretty colonial building. $$

COLONIA CONDESA

Condesa's 'Restaurant Row' clusters around the intersection of Michoacán and Tamaulipas. There are lots of attractive places to eat here, and the scene can be fun at night, but if you're after serious food, look beyond.

Duo Salado y Dulce *(Amsterdam 53 near Sonora, closed Mondays).* A Swiss baker runs this cozy place, popular for brunch. $$

Azul Condesa *(Nuevo León 68, near Laredo)* This upscale Mexican restaurant can be variable, but when it's good, it's great. $$$

Milos *(Amsterdam 308 at Celaya)* is a charming bistro with outdoor tables that look onto Av. Amsterdam; my favorite place for breakfast.$$

Felafelito Condesa *(corner of Chilpancingo at Parque México)* This hole-in-the-wall has very good felafel and fresh, safe-to-eat salad. $

El Tizoncito *(Tamaulipas 122 and Campeche 362, daily till midnight)* Go here for the most famous tacos al pastor in Mexico. Great salsas, too. $

Restaurante Taj Mahal *(Francisco Marquez 134, daily 2-10 p.m.)* You'll find the best Indian food in the city here. $$$

Fonda Mayora *(Campeche 322, open daily 8 a.m. -7 p.m. Tel. 6843-0595)* A hip, refined but traditional spot for breakfast or lunch. $$

COLONIA ROMA

Av. Álvaro Obregón is lined with restaurants and bars, which come and go with surprising speed. The food sometimes takes second place to the lively scene here. The following is a list of my favorite 'off the beaten track' eateries.

Yuban *(Colima 26B near Insurgentes)* offers country-style Oaxacan food in a stylish setting. The house-made tortillas and unusual mole dishes are excellent. $$

El Hidalguense *(Campeche 155)* Open for breakfast and lunch Friday - Sunday only, this family-style restaurant sports typical Mexican decor and friendly service. It's your best bet for classic barbacoa (pit-cooked lamb). $

Angelpolitano *(Puebla 371, near the corner of Sonora, closed Mondays)* This family run restaurant set in an old house specializes in Poblano (i.e. from Puebla) cooking. Their chile en nogada is the best. $$

Máximo Bistrot Local *(Tonalá 133 at Zacatecas, tel. 5264- 4291)* One of the best restaurants in all of Mexico. Chef Eduardo García is renowned for his careful attention to detail and all of his restaurants are worth a visit. Reservations in advance are a must. His **Lalo** across the street is great for breakfast or a light lunch, and **Havre 77**, (at the same adress, tel. 5208-1070) in nearby Colonia Juarez is classic French. Máximo, Havre, $$$, Lalo $

Rosetta *(Colima 166, Tel. 5533-7804)* Set in a lovely old mansion, award-winning chef Elena Reygadas does superb classic Italian food with a Mexican touch. Reservations are a must. $$$ Her **Panadería Rosetta**, *(Colima 179)* is a nice place for breakfast or a light lunch. $

El Axotleño *(Coahuila 152, 1 p.m.- 4 p.m.)* This economic comida corrida place, adjacent to the Mercado Medellín, is a notch above the rest.$

Pozolería Tizka *(Zacatecas 59, near Mérida)* The green pozole, thickened with pumpkin seeds, at this inexpensive local joint is one of the best things you'll eat in Mexico City. $

Bistro Broka *(Zacatecas 126, near Jalapa).* This neighborhood bar and restaurant serves an excellent up-scale comida corrida, and changes to tapas and wine at night. The backyard setting is pleasant. $$

Huset *(Colima 256, Roma, tel. 5511-6767)* is chef Maycoll Calderon's superb venue for simple grilled dishes, set in a lovely restored mansion.; I predict it will be the hottest spot in town before long. $$$

POLANCO

The hub of this area radiates from where Julio Verne meets Parque Lincoln. There are lots of fancy restaurants and a few fondas, making for a lively scene night and day.

Dulcinea *(Oscar Wilde 29, 9am-6pm)* offers creative Mexican food in a casual setting with outdoor tables. Good breakfast. $$

El Bajío *(Alejandro Dumas 7)* offers traditional Mexican food in a casual setting. It's famous for its carnitas (confit pork) but the mole is also great. A traditional Mexican breakfast is offered. $$

Anatol *(Masaryk 390 at Anatole France, 3300-3950)* Chef Justin Ermini brings American comfort food (and more) to Mexico City. It's the only place in the city to get a real pastrami sandwich. $$$

Dulce Patria *(Anatole France 100, 3300-3999)* Chef Martha Ortiz Chapa's neo-classic Mexican food is served with theatrical flair--it's a good place for a celebration dinner. $$$

Raiz *(Schiller 331)* Creative riffs on traditional Mexican ingredients works far better here than in most places of this type. $$$

ZONA ROSA

Once posh, but more recently down at the heels, this area is now home to a gay scene (Calle Amberes), a cluster of Korean businesses, and many chain restaurants. But there are some good places to eat as well.

Fonda El Refugio *(Liverpool 166)* This landmark Mexican restaurant serves high quality, very traditional recipes. The old house setting is cozy. $$

Casa de Toño *(Londres 144, open 24 hours)* For comida or late-night cravings for pozole, quesadillas, sopes. Popular, satisfying and inexpensive. $

Nadefo *(Liverpool 183)* This Korean restaurant is recommended by several community insiders. $$

Sole (General Prim 95) offers an oyster/raw bar and creative Baja. $$$

COYOACÁN AND SAN ÁNGEL

Most of the top restaurants are found around the main plaza in Coyoacán and along Avenida de la Paz in San Angel

El Rincon de la Lechuza *(Miguel Angel de Quevedo 34, near Insurgentes)* is a popular taquería, famed for it's tacos al pastor. $

Corazon de Maguey *(Plaza Jardín del Centenario 9A, Coyoacán)* overlooks the plaza and serves quality Mexican food as well as offering a huge selection of mezcales. $$

Taro *(Av. Universidad 1861, Coyoacán)* This popular 2nd floor spot offers traditional Japanese regional cuisine.$$

Taberna de León *(Altamirano 46, Plaza Loreto, tel. 5613 - 3951, San Angel)* This romantic restaurant is set in an old house within a paper mill converted into a shopping center. Renowned chef Mónica Patiño makes sure the kitchen keeps up the high standards. $$$

Street Stalls and Market Food

The term 'street food' often conjures up fear of Montezuma's revenge, and stops many people from trying some of the country's best cuisine. But in recent years, televison foodies like Anthony Bourdain have turned the term around, and eased the fears of many. Now street food, which includes that sold out of pushcarts, fixed stands called *puestos*, and market stalls, has become a hip catchword. Some of my favorite food in the city is street food.

There are also some very scary looking cauldrons of viscera floating in dark red sauces that could turn you into a vegetarian quickly. It took me several years to work up the courage to start eating food from street stalls because I assumed that all of it was greasy and loaded with bacteria. While there is no guarantee of germ-free food, even in fancy restaurants, I follow some basic guidelines when choosing where to eat.

Check out the stall and the cook for cleanliness. If it doesn't look clean, forget it. I choose food that I can see being cooked, and avoid anything that looks too greasy. I avoid deep fried items, unless I can see that the oil is clean and very hot. I don't eat what looks like it has been sitting outside for a long time. I look for crowded stalls that have been discovered by locals–they've already selected the good ones. Some vendors slip on a plastic glove before accepting money—a good sign. Make sure your own hands are clean before you eat. I carry a package of moist towelettes with me and use hand sanitizer that, these days, is often provided at street stalls.

The Best Street Food in Mexico City

The best street food is often found in and around markets and metro stops. You'll usually find a variety of stands offering everything from fresh fruit juices to savory tacos. Here's a list of my favorite street food spots around town.

Metro Chilpancingo *(Insurgentes and Baja California)* You'll find a line-up of food stalls near this metro stop, most on Calle Chilpancingo. Don't miss the excellent flautas, accompanied by a bowl of chicken soup.

El Taquetón (*at the corner of Baja California and Tuxpan*) is one of my favorite taco stands: try the tortitas of broccoli or cauliflower, rare vegetarian options.

Coyoacán Market *(Malantzín & Allende)* Besides its historical/cultural interest as the former haunt of Frida Kahlo, the main market of Coyoacán houses Tostadas de Coyoacan, one of the best and most visually spectacular market stalls in the city.

Polanco Tianguis *(Aristotoles & Luís G. Urbina, at the corner of Parque Lincoln, Saturdays only)* This cluster of appealing stalls proves that even in an upscale neighborhood like Polanco, folks love their street food.

Condesa Tianguis *(Agustin Melgar near Mazatlán, Tuesdays only)* There are many great street stalls: carnitas, barbacoa, tostadas, guisados, mariscos and quesadillas—and don't miss the mixiotes!

Jardín Pushkin Tianguis (*Colima and Morelia, Colonia Roma. Sundays only*) Locals line up for a space at the long tables here for classic antojitos, good seafood stalls.

Calle López (*Centro*) The blocks between the Salto de Agua metro stop and Calle Ayuntamiento is the ultimate place for street food in Mexico City.

Calle Mérida Tianguis (*Mérida near Chihuahua, Colonia Roma, Fridays only*) Local workers flock to this busy street market for classic Mexican antojitos, great pozole.

If you are hesitant about trying street food on your own, you can book a tour with local experts at http://www.eatmexico.com

Best Bars, Cantinas and Pulquerias

The line between a bar and cantina is a bit blurry; cantinas tend to be more down home and often offer food, sometimes free with drinks. Pulquerías only serve pulque.

CENTRO HISTÓRICO

Bar La Opera (*Cinco de Mayo 10*) This landmark place is a must see. But go for a drink, the food is lackluster.

Cantina Tio Pepe (*corner of Independencia and Dolores*) This 1870 cantina preserves its funky charm under decades of paint. It's the most atmospheric of the old cantinas, and a good place for a drink before going to Bellas Artes.

Pulquería Las Duelistas (*Aranda 30, near Ayuntamiento*) This is the best known of the old time pulquerías which have been repopulated with young hipster types.

Pulquería La Hortensia (*Plaza Garibaldi*) A classic old joint to have a drink while you listen to the mariachis on the plaza.

Miralto (*41st floor of the Torre Latinoamericana*) This is as high as you can get in the Centro for a drink or a meal. On a clear day the views are astounding.

Hotel Downtown *(Isabel la Católica 30)* The top floor terrace in this smartly remodeled colonial building is the hippest spot in the Centro.

ABOVE IT ALL: Rooftop Venues in Mexico City

With street life being so intense, it can be a great relief to head upwards and relax in a rooftop bar or restaurant, many of which afford spectacular views of the city.

Sears Café *(across from the Palacio de Bellas Artes)* On the 8th floor of art-deco Sears store you'll find a small café with a balcony overlooking the Palacio and its lovely manicured gardens.

Isabel la Católica 30, Located in a smartly remodeled colonial building, this new complex includes the Hotel Downtown & several restaurants and shops. The top floor terrace is a great place for a drink; you can use the pool for the price of a drink.

Miralto *(41st floor of the Torre Latinoamericana.)* This is as high as you can get in the Centro for a drink or a meal. On a clear day the views are astounding.

Several restaurants overlook the colonial splendor of the Zócalo, Mexico City's massive main plaza. Try **Puro Corazón** *(Monte de Piedad 11, 6th floor)*, or **Restaurant El Mayor** *(Republica de Argentina 15, corner of Justo Serra)* where you can contemplate the remains of the Templo Mayor.

Hotel Condesa DF *(Avenida Veracruz at Parque España, Colonia Condesa)*, the chic and trendy rooftop terrace is a great place for a drink, especially in March when the jacaranda trees are in bloom.

Bellini *(Word Trade Center, Colonia Napoles)* is the city's only revolving restaurant. It's tacky, but fun.

CONDESA AND ROMA

La Bodega *(Avenida Amsterdam 10, Colonia Condesa, Closed Sundays)* Good live Cuban music, and a homey atmosphere that feels like Greenwich Village in the '50's, keep this place ever popular. There is a small theater upstairs featuring local cabaret artists.

Condesa DF. *(Av. Veracruz at Parque España, Colonia Condesa)* The rooftop bar at this trendy and chic hotel is a great place at sunset or later. If the jacarandas are in bloom (March/April) don't miss it!

Covadonga *(Puebla 121 near Orizaba, Colonia Roma, Closed Sunday)* This traditional club for Spanish ex-pats has become a hangout for young artists--Thursday is the big night here. The wine list is good, food is fair: stick to basic tapas like tortilla española or tortas.

Licoreria Limantour *(Álvaro Obregón 106, Colonia Roma)* This is the most popular of the new trendy cocktail bars. **Baltra** *(Iztaccihuatl 28, Condesa)* is also hot

Expendio de Pulques Finos Los Insurgentes *(Insurgentes Sur 226, Colonia Roma)* Trendy Bar/pulquería set in a funky old mansion; they also offer light food.

COYOACÁN/SAN ANGEL

La Bipolar *(Malintzin 155)* This cool bar is owned by movie star Diego Luna. Light food is good.

La Guadalupana *(Higuera 14, off the main plaza, Coyoacán)* Frida and Diego supposedly hung out at this famous cantina, in operation since 1932. It offers good food.

POLANCO

Revés *(Virgilio 25)* This cool 'retro' bar is open Wednesday to Saturday

Surtidora Abarrotera Mercantil *(Julio Verne 93, near Parque Lincoln)* This is a 'contemporary cantina' with outdoor terrace for smokers.

Blue Lounge *(Hotel Camino Real, Mariano Escobedo 700, Anzures)* This bar, with its glass floor over a shallow pool, is the place for high heels and a slinky black dress.

SANTA MARIA DE LA RIBERA

Salón París *(Torres Bodet 152, corner Salvador Diaz Mirón)* This traditional, friendly cantina is supposedly the place where ranchera giant José Alfredo Jiménez got his start. Generous botanas are handed out free during comida hours.

What to See and Do

CENTRO HISTÓRICO

The Centro Histórico is Mexico City's oldest area and the best starting point for any visit. It is the hub of government, religion, and commerce, one of the liveliest and most beautiful parts of town. A massive earthquake heavily damaged the area in 1985, but recent investment is reviving the glamour that made it world famous in the 1950's, when the young Maria Callas sang at the Opera and Diego Rivera and Frida Kahlo dined at the Hotel del Prado (destroyed in the 1985 quake). The two most important areas to explore are the Zócalo and the Alameda. As you are walking around, be sure to look in every open door—the city is full of hidden surprises.

Palacio de Bellas Artes

WALKING TOUR #1:
The Route of Grandeur

This tour takes you on a loop, beginning and ending at the Zócalo, past some of the most magnificent architecture in the city, including Aztec ruins, Spanish colonial palaces, and "Porfiriato" commercial buildings.

☛ **Start your tour at the Zócalo.** Officially known as Plaza de la Constitución (although nobody calls it that) the Zócalo is the main square of Mexico City, one of the largest urban plazas in the world, and the political and religious center of the country since Aztec times. The Spanish name means pedestal: the story goes that a pedestal was put there by President Santa Ana in 1840, for a statue that never arrived. The name stuck and is now used to define town squares all over the country.

Arriving by metro gives you a dramatic first view of the Zócalo— you will exit right in the middle of it (use the exit marked Plaza de la Constitutión). If you hear drumbeats, follow the sound. You might encounter a group of *concheros*, men and women dressed in Aztec outfits who dance, chant, and burn incense in the plazas adjacent to the cathedral.

The Palacio Nacional

Groups of concheros are seen in many Mexican fiestas and parades, mixing the past and present. Dance steps represent astrological formations. Concheros often fast beforehand to intensify the near-trance state sought through the rhythms and motions of the dance. You may also see people lining up for a *limpia*, ritual cleansing using incense and herbs to get rid of bad spirits. You, too, can do this—just put a few pesos in the cup afterwards.

Concheros might strike you as commercial or kitschy (one Mexican friend calls them 'Plastic Aztecs'), pseudo-mystical or idealist, but judging by the widespread popularity, their brand of ethnic pride resonates here.

The Palacio Nacional (closed Mondays) covers the entire east side of the plaza and houses the office of the President. Moctezuma's palace was in this very spot. Surrounding the stairwell is the impressive mural by Mexico's most famous artist, Diego Rivera, entitled *Epic of the Mexican People*, painted between 1929 and 1935. It's a grand sweep of history with hundreds of individualized players, arranged in a masterful composition with a peacock's fan of colors. Upstairs are more Rivera murals (painted between 1941 and 1952) depicting the life

Diego Rivera mural, The Arrival of Cortés

of the Aztecs before the conquest. They are gorgeous and engaging, each one telling a story that is both public and private. The last mural depicts the Spanish conquistadores, shown in such an unflattering way as to leave no doubt about Rivera's opinions. In the middle of this last painting a young child, strapped to its mother's back, stares out at the viewer. This supposedly represents the first racially mixed *mestizo*, the child of Cortés and his consort, Malinche.

Guides are available to explain it all to you, but check that the one you hire speaks your language well—I've overheard some who were barely intelligible. There are public bathrooms on the ground floor.

The entrance/exit to the Palacio has been changed often, but currently you must leave the building on **Calle Moneda**, a beautiful street, almost completely lined with colonial buildings. Turn left as you exit to return to the Zócalo. On your right (Moneda 4) is the grand **Antiguo Palacio de Arzobispado**, the Catholic bishops' residence in colonial times, which has changing art shows.

The ruins of the **Templo Mayor**, the main site of Aztec worship, are to your right as you reach the Zócalo. Being in the midst of the temple ruins, in the heart of the modern city, is a rich and evocative experience, a compression of 700 years of history—all the more amazing when you realize the ruins  were only discovered in 1978 while electrical workers were laying new cables. The small museum displays art works from this site— the life-size ceramic warrior figures on the top floor are noteworthy.

Just next to the Templo Mayor is the massive **Catedral Metropolitana**, the most important Catholic church in Mexico. Begun in 1573, it was built using stones from the Templo Mayor. The smaller building on the right is the Sacristy, built almost 200 years later. The main Cathedral entrance brings you into the baroque splendor of the seat of Mexican Catholicism—lots and lots of gold. It is worth sitting down to view the main altar at the back of the church to absorb its baroque complexity.

If you're feeling adventurous you can take a tour of the rooftop domes and bell towers of the cathedral. Tours run every 20 minutes from 10 am to 4 pm daily. (Don't go in high heels!) You can get tickets at the table near the entrance.

As you leave the church go right along the tall iron railing. At the corner you'll see workers of many kinds, mostly electricians, plumbers, and brick masons lined up seeking employment for the day. There's an information kiosk on this side of the Cathedral with great maps. (There's also a taxi sitio and a Turibus stop on the left side of the Cathedral.)

Cross the street to **Avenida Cinco de Mayo**. Be sure to look up as you walk along to notice some of the best architectural details. At Palma 13 (first street on your right) the small balconies are a lovely detail of Porfiriato architecture, reflecting the French influence promoted by President Porfirio Díaz, dictator of Mexico between 1876 and 1911. As Victoria did in England, Díaz established a visual style for his country, which is strongly reflected in the Centro Histórico.

Two blocks from the Zócalo on Cinco de Mayo is **Jugos Canadá**, offering a wide assortment of refreshing fruit and vegetable drinks, like the ever-popular 'vampiros' made with beet and celery. The landmark **Café El Popular** (#52) serves excellent, inexpensive Mexican food— and it never closes.

Notice the muscle men supporting the Edificio Cantabria (#57). The Casa de Ajaracas (#46) and the Edificio Puebla (#43) are good examples of neo-colonial architecture, popular in the early 20th century. **Café La Blanca** (#40) has been around since the 1930's and displays photos on the wall to prove it; they serve good café con leche and service-able Mexican dishes from a large menu. The 19th century **Dulcería de Celaya** (#39), with its beautiful painted glass sign, sells traditional Mexican sweets, such as crystallized fruits and candies made from sweetened goat's milk. Try the limes stuffed with coconut—one of Frida K's favorites.

At the corner of Motolinia, notice the Aztec-Deco metal work at the **Edificio Banco Mexicano**. Zinco Jazz Club is in the basement of this building (enter at Motolinia 20).

Other elegant buildings of the Porfiriato period can be seen at #32 (Edificio París) and #20 (Edificio Cinco de Mayo).

At Cinco de Mayo 10 is the famous **Bar La Ópera**. There's not much to look at from the outside, so be sure to enter and see the beautiful wooden interior. The food is nothing special (stick to the appetizers), but it's a great place to stop for a drink and hear music played by musicians who seem as old as the bar itself. Ask to see the bullet hole in the ceiling left by Pancho Villa during the Revolution.

Further down Cinco de Mayo on the left is the back entrance to one of Mexico City's most famous and beautiful buildings, the **Casa de los Azulejos** (The House of Tiles). This 18th century aristocratic residence, whose facade is completely covered with tiles, is now the flagship **Sanborns.**

We'll get to the front entrance later in this tour, but for now, turn right on **Paseo de Condesa**—just across from the House of Tiles—and walk one block to Calle Tacuba and the **Plaza Manuel Tolsá** which features a statue of Charles V on horseback. On this small, but magnificent, plaza are the Palacio de Minería and the **Museo Nacional de Arte**, with a collection of Mexican art from colonial times to the 20th century. The entire plaza is the supreme example of Porfiriato architectural design. On weekends groups of concheros dance here.

Facing the museum, to your left on Tacuba, is the **Palacio de Correos**, Mexico's huge central post office. The eclectic architectural style and elaborate ironwork are impressive. Take the elevator up and walk down the grand staircase to appreciate the splendor.

As you leave the post office, go left along traffic-clogged Eje Central Lázaro Cárdenas, once lined with theaters and nightclubs (walk against the flow of traffic). You'll see the white wedding cake **Palacio de Bellas Artes** across the street. (This is described in the following Walking Tour of the Alameda, but if you don't have time for that tour, DO NOT miss seeing this building).

Go two blocks on Eje Central, crossing Cinco de Mayo and turn left when you reach pedestrian-only **Calle Madero**. On Madero, across from Sanborn's (the house of tiles), is the **Atrio de San Francisco**, a sculpture plaza with changing exhibitions. From this plaza you can enter the **Torre Latinoamericana**, inaugurated in 1956, an important symbol of modern Mexico, and until recently the city's tallest building. Ride up to the 44th floor *mirador* for the best aerial view of the city, or visit the bar/restaurant **Miralto** on the 41st floor (open daily, 2 pm-2 am tel. 5518-1710)—for a bit more than the cost of a mirador ticket you can get a drink and enjoy the view without the crowd.

Next to the sculpture plaza the **church of San Francisco** slowly sinks into the earth. It has one of the finest baroque facades in the city; the interior is less interesting. Walk up to the front door and look back for a

Casa de los Azulejos (Sanborn's)

beautiful view of the rooftop finials on the Casa de los Azulejos across the street.

Go into **Sanborns (Casa de Azulejos)** by its front door across from the church. It is worth spending a little time exploring this magical spot. The central patio is now a lovely dining area—a great place for breakfast or a light lunch. Go upstairs to see more of the tile work, and notice the ceiling over the staircase. There are clean public bathrooms, whose entrance is flanked by an **Orozco mural**. Sanborn's also sells a good selection of books, maps, magazines, and chocolates.

Exit Sanborn's the way you entered and turn left on Madero. At #17 is the **Palacio de Iturbide**, one of the finest colonial buildings in the city, built around 1780. Cross the street to fully appreciate its ornately sculpted facade. Once the home of the first president of the Republic, later a hotel, it is now owned by Banamex and is open to the public for changing free art exhibits of high quality. Try to get upstairs to see the small chapel on the right with its lovely dome.

At the corner of Madero and Isabel la Catolica are more fine examples of Porfirian architecture, including the **Museo del Estanquillo**, which has changing exhibits on Mexico City culture and history, and great views from the top floor café (free entry).

Turn right on Isabel la Católica and walk to #29 to visit the elaborate **Casino Español**, which now houses a restaurant and social club. Upstairs, the glamorous main salon facing the street is used for concerts and weddings.

Across from the Casino Español, check out the **Downtown Hotel** *(Isabel la Católica #30, www.downtownmexico.com)*, a chic renovation of a grand 18th century mansion, which now houses a hotel, two restaurants (OK, if not spectacular food) and several interesting shops on the mezzanine level. Don't miss the rooftop terrace, which has one of the city's hippest bars—and a small pool that you can use for a fee.

Head back and continue along Madero. You will pass lots of jewelry stores; at #74 is **Mumedi,** a trendy design store where you may find some gifts for the folks back home.

Madero ends at the Zócalo. On the right corner is the **Hotel Majestic**, whose fine neo-colonial lobby and rooftop restaurant are worth a look. Turn right at the Hotel Majestic and walk under the arcade, which dates back to 1524 and is the center of the jewelry business.

Turn right at the next corner (16 de Septiembre) and enter the **Gran Hotel de la Ciudad de Mexico** with its spectacular lobby and Tiffany stained glass ceiling—take the elevator to the 4th floor to get up close. The rooftop restaurant here has the best view of the Zócalo.

Gran Hotel de la Ciudad de Mexico, Tiffany stained glass ceiling.

Gran Hotel de la Ciudad de Mexico, rooftop view of the Zócalo.

From the hotel, walk away from the Zócalo along Calle 5 de Febrero one block to Calle Venustiano Carranza. Three of the corner buildings here, sporting round turrets, are **grand old department stores**. The Palacio de Hierro (sort of a budget version of Galeries Lafayette in Paris) still retains some of its old world splendor. Finished in 1891, it was Mexico's first iron and steel building, hence its name.

Turn left on Venustiano Carranza, and left again on 20 de Noviembre. Straight ahead is the Zócalo and a grand view of the Cathedral. If Mexico City can claim to have a 'front door', this is the spot.

The tour ends here.

WALKING TOUR #2:
The Alameda

This tour is a loop, beginning and ending at the Palacio de Bellas Artes—a walk around the park.

The Alameda, Mexico's most elegant park, dates back to colonial times, when only the rich were allowed to enter. The 2012 renovation erased some of the old time charm of the place with overly modern lighting and dancing fountains, but it's a great place to breathe in the oxygen, see the policharros (policemen on horseback wearing traditional Mexican garb), or get a shoeshine and just watch the world go by. The Alameda is especially nice in late afternoon when the sunlight streams through the trees and makes the fountains sparkle.

☛ **Start the tour at the Palacio de Bellas Artes**, the giant wedding cake that is Mexico's main venue for opera, concerts and ballet. Begun in 1904 in French Belle Époque style, the Mexican Revolution put a stop to construction. When things started again in the 1930's styles had changed, thus creating the surprising mixture of art deco with Aztec influence (notice the heads atop the lobby columns, a reference to the ruins of Teotihuacán). A dazzling **Tiffany glass stage curtain** and a glass dome inside the theater enrich the interior. If you cannot attend a performance, you can see the theater on a free tour (Spanish only), Monday through Thursday at 1 and 1:30 p.m.—ask at the information desk.

In the lobby, there is a pleasant restaurant and a bookstore with a good selection on Mexican art and culture. The museum upstairs features murals by Rivera, Tamayo, and Siqueiros, among others. **The Museum of Architecture** on the top floor is worth visiting for the views of the dome. You must buy a ticket in the lobby to go upstairs to either museum. On the plaza out front, don't miss the dark bronze statues, Los Pegasos, with their flying horses and ecstatic human figures.

If you're interested in attending a performance at Bellas Artes, check the listings on the wall in the front lobby, or ask at the information desk up the first flight of lobby steps. Ticket booths *(taquillas)* are near the entrance. The **Ballet Folklórico** stages colorful dance performances every Sunday and Wednesday.

Palacio de Bellas Artes

Directly behind Bellas Artes (Avenida Hidalgo) is the **Teatro Hidalgo**, which often has Broadway-type shows. On its left, down the block is the **Plaza de la Santa Veracruz**, flanked by two churches and two good museums. This plaza is both charming and disturbing as you see (once again) how the buildings are sinking into the soft ground below. In one corner of the plaza is the excellent **Museo Franz Mayer**, housed in a restored 16th century building. There's a permanent collection of decorative arts from the colonial period (the textiles are particularly good). Temporary exhibits, dealing with decorative arts and design, change every few months. The patio is one of the most charming spots in the city. If you don't wish to visit the museum proper, you can pay 5 pesos to enter the patio, where you'll find good coffee and light food.

On the same plaza is the **Museo de la Estampa**, a small museum devoted to printmaking, which has a long and honored history in Mexico.

At the far end of the Alameda on Hidalgo is the **Hotel de Cortés**, a grand colonial mansion that has been sleekly modernized, leaving it somewhat sterile, but the patio is still worth a peek.

Just beyond the park, across Reforma, you'll see the twin steeples of the **Ex-Convento de San Hipólito**, a church devoted to the worship of Saint Jude, patron saint of lost causes. Always busy, this place heats up on the 28th of each month, when hundreds of devotees arrive carrying huge statues of the saint to be blessed.

From the church, cross the wide intersection of Av. Hidalgo and Reforma, back to the Alameda (look for the big SEP sign). Walk along Balderas (where the Metrobús stops) one block to the **Plaza de la Solidaridad**, an extension of the Alameda. On the corner of this small plaza, you'll find the **Museo Mural Diego Rivera**, which houses his famous 'Dream of a Sunday Afternoon in the Alameda' from 1948. This colorful mural, filled with a 'who's who' of notable figures in Mexican history (including Rivera's wife Frida Kahlo), was formerly in the lobby of the Hotel del Prado, which collapsed in the 1985 earthquake. Miraculously, the mural survived unscathed and was moved to its current home, an impressive feat of engineering, which is chronicled inside.

A section of Dream of a Sunday Afternoon *in Alameda Park. 1947-48. Fresco, 15'9" x 49'3". Museo Mural Diego Rivera, Mexico City.*

Just around the corner at Juarez 89 (next to the Scientology building) is the **Fonart** store. This is the **Fondación Nacional de Artesanías**, a government-run store that features Mexican handicrafts from all regions of the country. Stock changes frequently, so you're never sure what you might find—but it's still one of the best places in town for good quality Mexican handicrafts. If you are visiting in October, the annual exhibition of prize-winning crafts is displayed upstairs—well worth it for serious collectors of Mexican folk art.

Cross Avenida Juárez, which runs along the south side of the Alameda (just look up and walk toward the high-rise **Hilton Reforma Hotel**— good clean bathrooms in the back of the lobby).

Take the first right past the hotel (Calle Revillagigedo) one block to the next corner (Independencia) and visit the **Museo de Arte Popular**. It houses an excellent collection of Mexican handicrafts, beautifully displayed, and a nicely stocked store. The Art-Deco building has been lovingly updated; be sure to notice the Aztec-style bas-relief decorations outside. Their website is *www.map.df.gob.mx*

After visiting the museum, head back to Avenida Juárez and turn right, walking toward Bellas Artes, parallel with the Alameda. You'll see a big white colonnade on the park side—the **Monument to Benito Juárez**, Mexico's most honored ex-president.

Directly across the street from the monument is **Patio Juárez**, an attractive new complex of government buildings, plazas and fountains designed by Ricardo Legorreta, architect of the Hotel Camino Real. The facade of a colonial church has been nicely incorporated into this plaza, which is used as an open-air art gallery. A striking modern building here, the Museo Memoria y Tolerancia, is devoted to the history of genocide.

Monument to Cuauhtemoc, last Aztec ruler.

A bit further down Juárez, directly across the street from the front of Bellas Artes, is a Sears store located in an art deco building. The 8th floor cafe is a great place to enjoy the view of the gardens below—and the coffee is good, too.

The tour ends here.

The nearest taxi sitio is across the park, at the corner of Hidalgo and Trujano (left of the Franz Mayer Museum). There are metro entrances behind Bellas Artes and at the corner of Tacuba and Lázaro Cárdenas.

LA RAZA

Past and present often inhabit the same space in Mexico City: the architecture, the food, the faces of the people, reveal mixed races and conquered tribes. Aztec place names abound: Tenochtitlán, Popocatepetl, Iztacíhuatl, Nezahualcoyotl, Chapultepec, Moctezuma (there are more than 800 Moctezumas in the Mexico City phone book).

Settled in 1325, it is the oldest city in the western hemisphere, a place founded on Aztec prophecy: an eagle, devouring a snake while perched on a cactus, was a messenger from the gods indicating the site of the city. This violent image, all thorns and claws, adorns the Mexican flag today.

Human sacrifice was among the rituals performed in their main temple, whose ruins you can see by the Zócalo, right in the midst of everything. When Hernán Cortés and his Spanish conquistadores took over in 1521, they used stones from this very temple to build their imposing cathedral next door.

Conchero dancers

Mexican Catholicism enveloped Aztec paganism, with statues and paintings graphically violent in ways rarely seen in European art. The basilica of La Vírgen de Guadalupe, the most revered religious site in all of Latin America, is built atop a shrine to the Aztec mother-goddess Tonantzín, and you will often find conchero dancers performing there in flamboyant Aztec costumes. In spite of the fact that Mexico is more than 90 percent Catholic, one senses the conversion is not complete and that traces of ancient beliefs are lurking in the shadows.

WALKING TOUR #3:
Let's Eat!

This tour takes you from the Zócalo to the Mercado San Juan, the gourmet market favored by local chefs, foodies, and foreigners, with stops at several of my favorite food stalls along the way. It passes through our little Chinatown and ends up at the Palacio de Bellas Artes.

☛ **Start at the southeast corner of the Zócalo** where Pino Suárez begins, in front of the Supreme Court Building. Across the street is the **Plaza Tenochitlán**, where a group of bronze sculptures commemorate the supposed spot where the city was founded.

From the Zócalo, walk three blocks south (direction of traffic) down Pino Suárez to the **Plaza Lic. Primo Verdad**. On the plaza itself is the Templo de Jesús Nazareno, a good, old fashioned Mexican restaurant, La Rinconada and a fabric store (look for Telas Para Cortinas) that will appeal to those who like to explore old houses.

But the main draw here is the **Museo de la Ciudad de México** (Pino Suárez 30), which has changing art shows, and an Aztec serpent's head as a foundation stone (corner of Calle el Salvador). The secret of this museum is upstairs—the **Estudio de Joaquin Clausell**, a cool, calm oasis in the center of the city. Clausell (1896-1935), an impressionist/symbolist painter, had his studio in this building owned by his wife's family. For years he used the walls as his sketchbook and the result is a delightful rambling mural of doodles, sketches and small paintings.

Continue on Pino Suárez two blocks further, passing lots of shoe stores, and turn right on **Calle Regina**, which becomes pedestrianized a block ahead. In 2007, this became the first street in the Centro to be closed to traffic, and what was once a dreary area is now filled with cafés, restaurants, a cultural center. There's more of a neighborhood feel here—on sunny days, for example, a ladies' crochet club meets across the way from the children's playground.

Three blocks ahead, at the corner of Regina and Isabel la Católica is **Café Jekemir**, which has the best coffee beans in town, and superb espresso. (Across the street at Isabel la Católica 83 is **Coox Hanal**, the top choice in town for Yucatecan food.)

Continuing along Regina you'll see a large wall of plants and the entrance to **Zéfiro**, a charming restaurant that is part of a culinary school—it's the most elegant dining option around here.

The cream-colored **church of Regina Coeli,** full of gilded altars, dominates the next plaza. Turn right here on Calle Bolívar, a street lined with stores selling musical instruments and sound equipment—usually very noisy. At #87 is **Casa Serra**, the best store in the city for art supplies. Walk a block to Mesones and turn left (a classic cantina, **La Mascota**, is across the street).

The street changes names to Vizcainas as it passes by the massive stone walls of the **Colegio de San Ignacio de Loyola**, the oldest continually operating educational institution in Mexico (not open to the public). The stones seem to be melting into the sidewalk here.

A block ahead you'll see wide, traffic-filled Eje Central. Cross the street, continue straight on Vizcainas, noting the art deco **Edificio Cosmos** and the **Cine Teresa**, a local landmark which can be seen in the opening sequence of Buñuel's iconic 1950 film Los Olvidados; sadly, its lobby is now a cell phone mall. A small branch of the Cineteca Nacional still shows movies upstairs, however.

One block past Eje Central, you'll reach **Calle López**. This is one of the great food streets of Mexico City, a veritable gourmet gauntlet. It's lined with humble family-run eateries and taco stands, and stores selling all sorts of kitchen supplies. This is *comida popular* (in its Mexican sense: of the people) at its best. Notice the hand-painted store fronts that add a touch of yesteryear to this colorful street.

(If you go two blocks to your left on Lopez you can visit the bustling **Mercado San Juan Arcos de Belén** -- not be to confused with the 'other' San Juan market later in this tour, but a great place to eat).

Head up López (against traffic) and join the line for meaty tacos at **Taquería González** (López at Vizcainas), or have an economical comida corrida at **La Gran Cocina Mi Fonda** at #51. At **Tacos Toluca** (corner of Puente de Peredo), try the green chorizo tacos. The seafood stands **El Caguamo** (three locations, all near Ayuntamiento) are local favorites.

Turn left off López when you reach Ayuntamiento (two blocks). On the next street to your left, Aranda, is the classic **Pulquería Las Duelista**s, with its Aztec fantasy murals, and **Molinera El Progreso** next door, which sells all kinds of nuts, seeds, and ground spices.

The **San Juan Artesanías market** on Ayuntamiento, on the left, is a bit forlorn these days but you may find a gift there. Just across the street is La Europea, a large wine and liquor store, and **El Huequito**, where you can sample the best tacos al pastor.

El Huequito, the best tacos al pastor in Mexico City.

Just past the craft market is a small leafy plaza framing a huge palm tree, guarded by the stately **1912 Buen Tono church**. This plaza is dedicated to famous radio personalities of the past, as the studio of Mexico's first station is down the block. Cut through the park diagonally toward the ominous space needle-like telephone tower. Go right at the far corner of the park—the street is called **Ernesto Pugibet**. Look up at the corner where a Chinese store is; you will see a sign for Cigarerros Mexicanos: this building housed a cigar and cigarette factory. Perhaps a Mexican 'Carmen' worked here.

The long blue wall here is the **Mercado San Juan**. From armadillos to zapotes, the range of foodstuffs will dazzle you. Professional chefs, serious cooks, and many foreigners shop here. Although not the most picturesque market, the selection of high-quality produce, fish and meat is unmatched in the city. There are a few small *comedores* (eating stands) in one corner, and a cheese stall offering great panini. For more information on this market, search **www.goodfoodmexicocity.com**, or visit the market's own website: www.mercadogourmetpugibet.com.

Mercado San Juan

Head back to Calle López and continue on (against traffic). Hardware and lighting stores take over the food stalls here, but there are some snazzy **art deco buildings** like the Edificio Victoria, #44, the Viena, #34, and the Rex, #28, which give clues to the former glamour of this neighborhood

At Artículo 123, turn left. This street specializes in parts to repair washing machines and blenders. Go one block and turn right on Dolores. You are now in Mexico City's *barrio chino*, the small **Chinatown**, founded by the Chinese immigrant community in the 1920's. There are no longer many Chinese here, just a few mediocre restaurants.

At the corner of Dolores and Independencia is one of my favorite classic cantinas, **El Tio Pepe**, full of funky, friendly ambience, cozy booths, and a beautiful mahogany bar.

The final block of Dolores before reaching the Alameda becomes more 21st century, with modern looking eateries offering sushi, pizza, and baguettes. At the end of the street you'll see the park and the **Palacio de Bellas Artes**

The tour ends here.

The nearest taxi stand is at the Hilton—go left down the Alameda. Turning right, the Zócalo is eight blocks straight ahead.

TRADITION IN THE CENTRO:
La Pastelería Ideal

The aroma gets you about fifty feet from the door, a warm mixture of sugar and butter combining with the exhaust fumes from nearby Eje Central. As you pass through the doors of the Pastelería Ideal you enter a life-size version of Candyland. Thousands of sugary cakes, muffins, tarts, strudels, danish, biscuits, croissants, éclairs, cream puffs, donuts, cupcakes and brioche are spread out before you; more than 300 varieties. And that's not including the cookies (I counted almost 70 different kinds).

A beloved institution known to generations of Mexicans, it was founded by Spanish immigrant Don Adolfo Fernández Cetina in 1927. He came to Mexico City in 1913 at the age of 17 to work with a cousin in his small bakery business. Today there are three locations in the city with more than 250 employees. The ovens are going 24 hours a day, seven days a week.

Need a cake to feed 1600? No problem. You could bake it at home (all you need is 100 kilos of flour, 400 eggs, 40 kilos of butter, and a 10-foot ladder to reach the top), or head upstairs to Ideal's **second floor cake showroom**. You'll see hundreds of cakes of all sizes, shapes and colors—the biggest, with nine layers, requires three workers to construct. Decorations might include a plastic lucha libre doll, ice cream cones, or even a tiny ballerina twirling above a bubbling fountain with twinkling lights.

There are cakes for weddings, *quinceañeras* (a girl's 15th birthday), birthdays, baptisms, and graduations. Ideal has provided cakes for TV and movie stars as well as for four Mexican presidents.

Are the cakes on display real? Furtive finger marks in the frosting certainly suggested they might be. It turns out the frosting is real—egg whites and sugar—but the cake itself is Styrofoam. "They last for years, but they'll get dirty, so we replace them every month or so," an employee told me.

How to shop in a Mexican bakery:
Pick up one of the metal trays and a pair of tongs and help yourself. At Ideal, go to the counter in the back of the store where you will be given a ticket with the price written on it. Pay at the *caja*, then go back to the counter where your wrapped pastries await you.

Pasteleria Ideal, *Calle 16 de Septiembre 18,* is open from 6 am to 10 pm daily.

WALKING TOUR #4:
From the Zócalo to the Merced and Sonora Markets

This very old area of the city was once intersected by canals and has always been a center of commerce. It's funky, noisy, and crowded—and builds to a crescendo at two of the cities bustling markets, Merced and Sonora. Do this walk in the morning around 10 am as things can get uncomfortably crowded in the markets after noon, especially on weekends.

☛ **Start at the southeast corner of the Zócalo** walking down **Corregidora Josefa Ortiz de Dominguez**—the **Palacio Nacional** is on your left. Street vendors boldly sell their pirate goods in the shadow of the Palacio. Notice how everything is spread out on blankets with loops at each corner, ready for a quick getaway in case of a police raid. Walk straight ahead on Corregidora.

At the corner of Jesús María, look up and notice the worn *hornacina*, a corner niche for a saint's statue, a common feature of colonial architecture in this area.

At the corner of Roldán is **La Peninsular**, which claims to be the oldest cantina in the city (1872). Turn right on Roldán. At #16, on the left, you'll see the **Café Equis** with its charming hand painted signs, and coffees from around the world.

Turn left at Manzanares and walk straight until you see the dollhouse like **Capilla del Señor de la Humildad**, which marked the city limits in the 16th century. Today it is known as the place where local thieves and prostitutes come to pray.

Just past the church, turn right onto busy, wide **Anillo Circunvalación**, a funky commercial street that will lead you to the Merced. A few blocks ahead, across the street, is the **Church of Santo Tómas**, with its broad front patio—it's cool, austere interior is your last chance for peace and quiet in this part of town.

Just past the church turn left. Looking up you'll see some lacy grille work on a building straight ahead—that's the main building of **La Merced**, the city's biggest retail food market. Against the front wall of the building is a row of food stalls selling classic *antojitos*. Once you

Dried chilies at La Merced market.

enter, you are in a vast world of fruit and vegetables—I have foodie friends who have spent hours here. Look for the sign indicating *desnivel*, a ramp that will take you to a lower level where you'll find craft items such as baskets, brooms, and toys and a passageway that leads to the meat and fish building.

The street between these two buildings, Rosario, will lead you to the **Sonora Market**—just ask any vendor if you're confused. Follow Rosario until you see a pedestrian bridge ahead of you. The Sonora Market is just across the bridge. This market is sometimes called 'The Witches' Market' since it's where you can find everything you need to cast a spell to get rich, fall in love, eliminate gossip, or regain your health. Herbs, ointments, candles, and incense, strange roots, shells, and all sorts of lucky charms are for sale. Head for Pasillo 8 (on the far left as you face the market) to see the best selection.

The tour ends here.

I find after a visit to this market area I always need a nap. The nearest metro stop is near the front of La Merced.

WALKING TOUR #5:
Through Seven Plazas — A Walk on the Wild Side

☞ *This walk takes you north, behind the Cathedral, to areas rarely visited by tourists, but full of colonial architecture, busy commercial streets, churches, markets, plazas and even a synagogue. It's less glamorous here, but very lively. I've never felt unsafe here, but I suggest you leave your Rolex at home.*

Start directly behind the cathedral on República de Guatemala, the street that runs parallel to its back wall. It is lined with colonial buildings, several of which are adorned with lacy *ajaracas* (bas-relief patterns). The **Centro Cultural de España** at #18 has changing art exhibits and a lovely rooftop café.

Walk through the *pasaje* (passageway) at #10, which is filled with statues of saints and all kinds of religious paraphernalia, and shops offering traditional curative herbs.

You'll exit on Calle Donceles. Half a block to your right, and across the street, is the **Templo de la Enseñanza**, whose peaceful interior is one of the finest examples of Mexican baroque. It's a perfect place to absorb the tranquil energy you will need on this walk.

Walk back down Donceles (against the flow of traffic) to Calle República de Brasil and turn right.

One block ahead on Brasil is the stately **Plaza Santo Domingo**, surrounded by imposing colonial buildings. At #31 you can enter the SEP building to see some of the **best murals of Diego Rivera** (see p. 80). Across the plaza, under the arcades, public scribes work at their typewriters, amid small printing businesses still using handset type. You can have business cards made here and pick them up a few hours later.

At the far end of the plaza is the **Church of Santo Domingo**, with several gilded baroque altars. At the corner of República Venezuela is the imposing **Antiguo Palacio de la Inquisición**, now a museum of medicine (free), with scary bottled fetuses and even scarier photos of plastic surgery. Note the 'missing' columns in the corners of the main patio.

Poster for Lucha ibre at the Arena Coloseo.

Continue along Brasil (on the right side of the church), looking up at the lumpy statue of the Virgin next to the funky Hotel Río de Janiero (#45), and the ornamental excess of the apartment building at the next corner, Bolívar.

Turn left when your reach República de Perú, noticing the *hornacina* atop the building across the street. These niches for statutes of saints are a common feature of colonial buildings in this part of town.

At the end of this block (Peru 77) is the **Arena Coloseo**, the oldest lucha libre stadium in the city (see p.170 for more about this peculiar form of Mexican wrestling).

Just past the Arena Coloseo, turn right on República de Chile. You are now in a fashion fantasy land, with store after store selling flamboyant dresses and accessories for weddings, *quinceañeras,* and other festive occasions.

One block ahead, turn right on República de Honduras, where the dresses seem to become even more outrageous and the street becomes more derelict.

Just as the city seems to be decaying around you, the lovely **Plaza de Santa Catarina** comes into view. Past the church, the street changes name from Honduras to República de Nicaragua. Continue straight, lamenting glory lost.

A block ahead is the intersection of República de Argentina (don't turn), which is completely clogged with street vendors. The infamous **Tepito neighborhood** is off to the left here—don't go here at night! Continue straight along Nicaragua. The **Templo de Nuestra Señora del Carmen**, although half-hidden by taco stands, offers a moment of tranquility. The street ends one block ahead, where you will turn right. Ahead of you is the **Plaza del Estudiante**, essentially invisible under the mass of wholesale merchandise on display.

You'll be in the midst of street vendors hawking all kinds of plastic stuff, mostly from China. You're not likely to do a lot of shopping here, but the street theater is great. The best way to appreciate this commercial chaos is as an abstract display of light, color and sound. Don't try to rush through—take time to feel this quintessential Mexico City moment. It's alive! I like to imagine that the rhythms of the vendors' calls were just the same in Aztec times—stop and listen.

The street jogs a bit and changes name to Carmen—lots more street vendors here. At #69 is the landmark **restaurant El Taquito**. Just past that, turn left on Bolivar, a street lined with cuddly stuffed animals. Straight ahead, you'll see the bell tower of the **Templo de San Sebastian**, which dates back to the 1500's when this was an Aztec neighborhood. Across from the church is the **Plaza Torres Quintero**, a scruffy spot that retains just a hint of its colonial past.

Just past the church, turn right and walk along Calle Rodríguez Puebla. A block ahead on your right is the **Mercado Abelardo Rodríguez**, one of the city's oldest market buildings, built in the 1920's, a traditional neighborhood market, it is best known for the entryway murals by students of Diego Rivera, including Isamu Noguchi, now shamefully neglected.

A block beyond the market (still on Rodríguez Puebla) is **Plaza Loreto**, which has recently been refurbished and cleared of street vendors. The magnificent, albeit crumbling, church boasts the largest dome in Latin America.

Directly across the plaza from the church is a **synagogue**, built in 1923 and one of the few remaining traces of the Jewish community that once inhabited the Centro. You can arrange a tour through their website *www.sinagogajustosierra.com.*

As you face the synagogue, go left on Mixcalco, past the National School for the Blind, then right on Leona Vicario. A block ahead is the **Plaza de la Santísima** and just beyond the plaza, the baroque masterpiece **Templo de la Santísima Trinidad**; check out that ornate front portal.

Sinagoga Justo Sierra.

Turn right at the church plaza, climbing up the ramp or the stairs to reach Calle Gral. Emiliano Zapata (which changes its name one block ahead to Calle Moneda—don't blame me!). At the corner of Jesus María you may notice a skeleton like female statue—this is **Santa Muerte,** patron saint of thieves and drug dealers. Stop for a moment at the corner of Moneda and Academia to take in the architectural splendor, and notice how little must have changed here in the past 200 years.

Within a block of this spot are several museums you could visit, if you have the energy. All of them are in fine colonial buildings: the **Museo José Luís Cuevas** (Academia 13), the **Casa de la Primera Imprenta** (Moneda 6), the **Museo Nacional de las Culturas** (Moneda 13), and the **Casa de Antiguo Arzobispado** (Moneda 4).

You'll reach the Zócalo, the seventh plaza on this tour, one block further along Moneda.

The tour ends here.

OTHER RECOMMENDATIONS IN THE CENTRO

Secretaría de Educación Pública *(enter from Plaza Santo Domingo 31)*. Some of the most beautiful murals by Diego Rivera are here—more intimate that the grand tableaux in the Palacio Nacional, and there is never a crowd. There is a lot to see, so I recommend that you start upstairs on the 3rd floor. The murals here were painted later than those on the ground floor and show a firmer compositional technique and mastery of color. They are perfectly fitted to the architecture: a long scroll with words from songs of the revolution unites the many small murals. There are clean bathrooms here on all floors. If you are visiting in March, you will see a fine display of jacaranda blossoms in the back patio.

Antiguo Colegio de San Ildefonso *(Justo Sierra 16, behind the Templo Mayor)*. This former Jesuit school dates back to the 16th century. Today it is one of the city's finest museums, with changing exhibits, always of high quality. There's an early mural by Rivera and several by Orozco here, and the building alone is worth the visit. *(Free on Tuesdays, closed Mondays)*.

Museo Nacional de Arte *(Tacuba 8)*. Set on a narrow but majestic neo-classic plaza, this 1905 building houses the best collection of Mexican art in the city from the 17th to the 20th century, with temporary exhibits, usually of well-chosen contemporary art on the first floor. Noteworthy are the 19th-century landscape paintings of José Maria Velasco and the woodblock prints of José Guadalupe Posada. Check out the cast-iron staircase, too.

Festival de Centro Histórico: Each year at springtime there is an international festival of cultural events at various venues throughout the Centro, lasting several weeks.

Check their website *www.festival.org.mx*

Frida Kahlo's paintings have shown the world a slice of Mexican surrealism: *Reality is not so different.*

One Friday afternoon I went to see an exhibit by Gabriel Orozco, a well-known contemporary artist, whose conceptual works are shown in museums around the world. Nick and I were the only two people there. Leaving the gallery (less than impressed by the cluster of battered soccer balls on display), we were walking along Paseo de la Reforma and saw a group of about twenty people looking up and pointing toward the sky.

I asked what was going on. "It's a UFO," I was told, but looking up could see nothing but a beautiful blue sky streaked with cirrus clouds. With more help from a bystander I finally saw the miniscule white dot, but was baffled by how anyone could have seen it in the first place. A block away at the busy intersection of Insurgentes, Nick noticed that a man was removing his pants. Suddenly dozens of men were removing their pants and shirts. Soon hundreds were standing on the sidewalk in their underwear, pulling them down to expose their butts to passing traffic. Next to the statue of Cuauhtémoc (leader of the Aztecs after Moctezuma) nine rather fleshy women were removing all of their clothes and painting slogans on their bodies with white paint. It turned out to be a protest against the corruption of the governor of the state of Veracruz. No one seemed surprised but us.

Once in the Zona Rosa, a touristy area of restaurants, shops and offices, I saw that someone had made their home—a corrugated metal shack —on an abandoned lot between two high-rise buildings, while the rest of the property had been turned into a corn field. A late-night TV variety show I watched included segments about the Virgin of Guadalupe, erectile dysfunction, and a reading of poetry by Octavio Paz, all immediately followed by an advertisement for bullet-proof windows for your car. Mexico is the capital of the unexpected.

WALKING TOUR #6:
Beyond the Centro—The Oldest Barrios

This tour takes you through Colonias Tabacalera, San Rafael, and Santa María La Ribera.

These barrios were the first planned expansions beyond the Centro, dating back to the early 1800's, built to accommodate Mexico's growing affluent class. By the 1940's all of these areas had begun their slow decline, mansions falling into disrepair or torn down to make way for cheap housing. But there are still many architectural gems to be found here.

Now, after decades of neglect, a new wave of young artists and entrepreneurs are shaking things up. These are all 'up and coming' neighborhoods, with signs of new life sprouting from the decay.

☛ **Start the tour in Colonia Tabacalera at the Plaza de la República**, whose centerpiece is the **Monumento a la Revolución Mexicana** *www.mrm.mx/eng*), with its massive copper-clad dome. The original design was part of a huge project for the Mexican Parliament, but construction was interrupted by the Revolution. When things finally settled down, it was decided to use the structure as a war memorial, finished in 1936, which explains its art deco influence.

The plaza itself is surrounded by large, impersonal government buildings, the only standout being the big yellow art deco Fronton Mexico building—a former jai-alai stadium closed in the 1970's and still awaiting renewal. After years of neglect, the plaza was gussied up in 2010 with the addition of playful fountains and a glass elevator that whisks you up to the top of the dome.

Buy a ticket for the *mirador*, which opens at noon, to see the city views—the structure itself is just as fascinating.

The museum below will appeal to history buffs who read Spanish, but kids will be bored stiff.

Go straight as you exit the monument, heading toward the palm trees. There are some good food stalls on your right, including **Tacos Memín**, named after a popular and rather un-PC cartoon figure.

Monumento a la Revolución Mexicana

Crossing Av. Insurgentes, you enter **Colonia San Rafael**, one of the first planned neighborhoods outside the Centro Histórico, catering to the wealthy class in the 19th century. Although there are still almost 400 buildings here classified as having 'historical value', the sense of decline predominates. Many of the old buildings are now schools or offices. There's still a feeling of a neighborhood here, but it's often overshadowed by the commercial influx. Recently, a few art galleries have opened and artists looking for cheaper studio space are moving in.

After crossing Insurgentes you'll be on Calle Gómez Farías, lined with street food stalls. At the first intersection, Sardi Carnot, you can see one of the grandest mansions of the area to your left. It is now the Universidad del Valle de Mexico (open only to students).

Turn right on Sardi Carnot, which has more of a neighborhood feel. One block ahead, turn left on to Thomas Alva Edison, noting the **grand old houses** at #160 and #162.

Continue two blocks and turn right on Serapio Rendón, a street where the sense of neglect and decay works up to a crescendo at the spectacular but abandoned **Cine Ópera**, a movie palace inaugurated in 1948.

To the right of the Cine Opera is the lovely colonial-era **Parroquia de San Cosme y San Damian**, where neighbors come to pray and enjoy a moment of silence.

The wide, busy street, Ribera de San Cosme, is just past the church. In 2013, hundreds of street vendors were "relocated" from here, taking what little life there was out of this dismally ugly thoroughfare. Cross this street and head right, walking two blocks to Dr. Enrique González Martinez and turn left.

You have now entered **Colonia Santa María la Ribera**. I recently saw a sign advertising a new apartment building here, billing the colonia as *'The New Condesa'*. It has a long way to go to compete with its fashionable neighbor to the south, but as would-be city dwellers get priced out of other neighborhoods, we're bound to see this once-charming area gain new life.

A few hundred feet ahead on Dr. Martinez you'll see the grand **Museo del Chopo** on your left (*www.chopo.unam.mx,* closed Mondays). This 1903 cast-iron building, which resembles a Parisian train station, is Mexico's answer to London's Crystal Palace—a marvel of engineering and design. It is now a contemporary art exhibition space.

As you leave the museum, go left on Dr. Martinez one block, and then left again on Amado Nervo. Two blocks ahead, turn right on Santa Maria la Ribera, the 'Main Street' of this colonia. Taco stands, tamal vendors, and mom-and-pop stores with hand painted signs give this street a cozy feel. At #52 listen to the squeaky sound of tortilla presses—one of those archetypal sounds that defines a Mexico City neighborhood. The Edificio Vigil, at #112, is a fine example of neo-colonial architecture.

Note: If you are here on a Thursday, be sure to take a brief detour on Ramon L. Velarde to visit the weekly tianguis (street market).

Continue along Santa Maria la Ribera until it ends (three blocks), at which point you will be facing the **Alameda**, the area's central plaza, with its grandly gaudy **Kiosko Morisco**, a Moorish fantasy pavilion originally built for a 1886 world's fair in New Orleans and later moved here.

Kiosko Morisco

On the near left corner of the Alameda is the **Salon París**, a friendly cantina serving decent food, where famed Mexican singer/songwriter José Alfredo Jiménez got his start.

Museo de Geología

On the far left corner of the Alameda, up from the Salon París, is the **Museo de Geología** *(closed Mondays),* one of the most elegant buildings in all of Mexico City—the time-warp interior could be a set for a Steven Spielberg movie. The grand cast-iron staircase leads up to a landing decorated with paintings and stained glass panels by famed 19th-century artist José María Velasco, whose panoramic landscape paintings can be seen in the Museo Nacional. *(The staircase is usually roped off, but if it's not busy and you ask nicely, they may let you go up.)*

Continue clockwise around the plaza—a mish-mash of old and new—until you reach Calle Salvador Díaz Mirón. Surprisingly, there's a Russian restaurant, Kolobok, on the corner, run by real Siberians—it's a local landmark, but the food is dull.

Turn left on Díaz Mirón—a street that pretty well encapsulates the ups and downs of this colonia—and walk three blocks to Av. Insurgentes.

Cross the green pedestrian bridge and enter the **Centro Commercial Forum Buenavista**—a glitzy new shopping mall/train station that wonderfully contrasts with what you've just been walking through. If the sun is right, there's a good view of the city from the top floor.

Veer to the far right of the lobby, following the signs 'Salida Buenavista' and head out to the street. On your left is the **Biblioteca Vasconcelos,** Mexico City's newest public library. Don't let the rather staid exterior keep you from entering what is perhaps the most spectacular library you'll ever see.

The tour ends here.

There are several Metrobús stops here, and a taxi sitio across the street, in front of the Suburbia store.

ADDITIONAL INFO:

The best place to eat in Santa María la Ribera is **La Casa de Toño,** *Calle Sabino 166,* two blocks west of the Alameda. Pozole and classic Mexican snacks are served in a restored mansion; prices are more than reasonable.

The nearby **Museo de San Carlos,** *(Avenida Puente de Alvarado 50—closed Mondays)* makes a good addition to a tour of this area. It is housed in a lovely former mansion, designed by Manuel Tolsá, with a small but classy collection of European art, including several works by Zurburán and a quirky Pontormo. There is a quiet café in back.

Pozole

AMIGOS

To say that Mexicans are warm and friendly is hard to deny. People are polite, often kind, and always patient. Modes of etiquette and social behavior exist in Mexico that have disappeared, or never existed, in many societies. When entering a store, for example, exchanges of *buenos días* or *buenas tardes* are obligatory, and upon leaving one often hears *que le vaya bien*, literally, "may it go well to you." In restaurants you will hear strangers saying to one another *buen provecho* (like "bon appétit"). Men shake hands upon meeting, and hugging is common among friends. It is customary for men and women friends to kiss cheeks, sometimes even upon first introduction. Young lovers in parks and metros are openly affectionate; couples in restaurants will sit next to, not across from, one another. References are made to physical qualities as terms of endearment. Anyone with light hair or skin will be called *güera* (or *güero* for men). Chubby friends will be called *gordo* or *gorda*. An African-American friend of mine is callled *negrita* ("little black girl") when she shops in the market. Spanish spoken in Mexico reflects this tenderness with the softening use of the diminutive *-ita* or *-ito* after many nouns, as when a waitress once offered me "*azucarcito para mi cafecito*" (little sugar for my little coffee). Once you get used to this warm social lubrication, much of the rest of the world seems cold indeed.

WALKING TOUR #7:
From the Centro to Colonia Roma

This tour takes you from the edge of the Centro through Roma Norte. It's a mixture of glamour, decay and history—in other words, Mexico City.

☛ Start the tour at the front door of the **Lotería Nacional** *(Paseo de la Reforma #1)*, a grand art deco building finished in 1945. From this plaza you can see some of the most iconic structures in Mexico City—the Torre Latinoamericana, the Monumento de la Revolución, the big yellow 'El Caballito' statue, and (on a clear day) way down Reforma, El Ángel de la Independencia. The Lottery building has an imposing front door and bronze panels on each side representing the goddess Fortuna.

Cross the plaza and walk towards the gaudy Carl's Jr. Burgers. This is the Esquina de la Información, where several of the city's largest newspapers have their offices, and the beginning of **Avenida Bucareli**.

Bucareli was once one of the city's grandest boulevards. In her 19th century memoir, Madame Calderón de la Barca noted the comings and goings of local aristocracy along this street. Some of its finest existing buildings date from the early 20th century, but the current grandeur sits next to some of the worst urban decay in the city.

Two blocks down (at Morelos) is the landmark **Café La Habana**, a 1950's era hangout for journalists and intellectuals (Fidel Castro was reportedly a regular during his stay here).

Straight ahead in the middle of the street is the clock tower known as the **Reloj Chino**, a gift from the emperor of China in 1910. On your left is the **Edificio Gaona**, a gem of neo-colonial architecture built in the 1920's—now full of squatters. It is best appreciated from across the street, in front of the grand neo-classic **Secretaría de Gobernación building**. The dilapidated building next door is a startling constrast.

The 1912 **Edificio Vizcaya** (Bucareli 128) is a huge apartment building that has not lost its cachet (the friendly doorman might let you peek into the courtyard).

Lotería Nacional on the left, and the the big yellow 'El Caballito' statue on the right.

Down the block (where Calles Tolsá and Barcelona intersect Bucareli), the four corner buildings date to the 1930's, but are practically buried beneath gaudy commercial signage (notice the bas-relief details on Barcelona 3F).

A block further, on your right, is the **Edificio La Mascota**, a complex of apartments occupying an entire square block built in 1912 to house workers for a now-defunct cigar factory. It's a fine example of the French-influenced architecture of the period.

Just beyond that, on the right, is the **Mercado Juárez**, a typical neighborhood market, a good place for a cheap 'comida corrida', but not one of the most picturesque markets in town.

Cross the wide Avenida Chapultepec (toward KFC) and continue down Bucareli (which now changes its name to Avenida Cuauhtémoc). You'll pass a shopping mall on your right, which houses the **Centro Cultural Telmex** on the second floor, a theater which often stages Spanish versions of Broadway musicals (usually quite well done).

Continue straight, crossing Calle Puebla, go one more block along Cuauhtémoc and turn right on **Real de Romita**.

You are now in the area known as **Romita**. *This little enclave, tucked into the northeast corner of Colonia Roma, has roots in pre-Hispanic times, when it was called Aztacalco. One block ahead is the tiny Church of* **Nuestra Señora de la Natividad**, *which dates back to the 16th century—but the colorful street murals along the narrow length of Callejón de Romita (behind the church) are pure 21st century. The small plaza features a (sometimes) bubbling fountain and cast-iron benches, all shaded by a few old trees. There is a strong sense of pueblo here, far removed from the hip and trendy scene of nearby* **Colonia Roma** *(which was named after Romita). The area used to have a rough reputation: it was used as a set for Buñuel's 1950 classic film of urban struggle, Los Olvidados.*

From the church plaza, follow Callejón San Cristóbal and go left on Morelia, then continue two blocks until you reach Colima. On your left is **Jardín Pushkin**, which has a lively tianguis on Sundays, offering great street food. The hamburger stand on the corner 'Burgers a la Parilla' is a neighborhood favorite, popular as a cure for hangovers.

Go right on Colima. **Abarrotes Delirio** (Colima 114 near Merida) is a great place to stop for coffee and light food. Next door to that is a cupcake shop, a sure sign that you have entered the trendy area of Colonia Roma.

Notice the leafy passageway at Colima 125 and the tiles on #123, the shells and medallions at #100 and the group of old houses #89 to 93.

The food stalls in front of the Sumesa grocery store are always busy—a good place to sample quesadillas or sopes.

This is the heart of Colonia Roma Norte where you may hear some typical neighborhood sounds—the whistle of the knife sharpener, the bell of the garbage collectors, or the cry of the tamal vendors. The area still retains the flavor of its past, in spite of having become a magnet for all things hip and trendy in recent years.

At Colima 145 (corner of Córdoba) is **MODO**, the Museo del Objeto del Objeto, which offers changing shows of 'everyday objects' that are usually quite intriguing. The building is one of the few examples of Art Nouveau architecture in the city.

After visiting the museum, continue on Córdoba (walking against traffic), stopping at **Artes de México** (Córdoba 69), which has a small but smart gift shop. Try to sneak upstairs to see the elegant offices in this former mansion.

At the end of the block, turn left on Durango. The **Antiguedades San Cristóbal** shop near the corner often looks closed, but ring the bell if you're interested in good quality Mexican crafts and antiques.

Straight ahead on Durango is **Plaza Río de Janeiro** with its reproduction of Michelangelo's David standing in a fountain. It's a nice place to hang out and watch the world go by.

Around the plaza are two worthy **art galleries** (OMR and Arróniz, on opposite corners of Durango), the famous Edificio Brujas (across from OMR), and, tucked into the far left corner of the plaza, one of the prettiest houses in Roma, with purplish walls and lovely sculpted garlands.

The tour ends here.

There is a taxi sitio on the corner of Durango and Jalapa, one block from this plaza. Turning left on Orizaba will take you to Av. Álvaro Obregón, the main commercial street of Colonia Roma.

MODO, the Museo del Objeto del Objeto.

WALKING TOUR #8:
Through the Colonias — Roma to Colonia Juarez

☞ **This tour starts where the previous one ends, at Plaza Rio de Janeiro** in Colonia Roma, which is described above. It continues through Roma Norte to the Zona Rosa, Colonia Juárez, and ends at the Monumento de la Revolución in Colonia Tabacalera, (where Tour #6 starts).

From **Plaza Río de Janeiro**, head north on Orizaba (David's front side). At Orizaba 37 is a branch of the famous **Dulcería de Celaya**, where you'll find classic Mexican candies. At the next corner, Puebla, is the Church of the Sagrada Familia, an eclectic, early 20th century building. Diagonally across from the church is the **Casa Universitaria del Libro**, part of the national university system. Be sure to check out the glamorous lobby staircase and stained glass in this former private mansion.

Turn left on Calle Puebla (in the direction of traffic), and go two blocks to reach Insurgentes—then turn right. Notice the string of once-lovely Porfiriato houses across Insurgentes, practically submerged by commercial dross.

A block ahead is the **Glorieta de Insurgentes**, a huge traffic roundabout and the entrance to the metro. You'll go up a few steps, passing Erik Mar, a store selling sexy drag queen style clothes, which sets the tone for this tacky, fabulous bit of the city. Just past the store, walk down the stairs to enter the glorieta. Hang out, get your shoes shined, and notice the wall relief tiles using pre-Hispanic motifs at the metro entrance.

Across the circle from where you entered, take the exit marked 'Genova'. You are now in the **Zona Rosa**, a lively commercial area of city, whose glamorous heyday of the 1940's is long gone. It has improved over the past few years from its descent into the sleazy realm of table dance bars, and now has many international chain restaurants and tourist-oriented stores. It may all look familiar, making it one of the least surprising parts of Mexico City. But somehow its fame as a social hot-spot lingers on.

From Genova, go left on Calle Londres. In the lobby of the **Hotel Géneve**, once the hotel of choice for the bohemian set, you might want to stop at the Phone Bar. Just outside the bar is an old telephone, where you can hear the voice of President Porfirio Díaz talking to Thomas Edison—Mexico's first sound recording! Lots of other interesting memorabilia here, too.

At Londres 144 is is a branch of **Casa de Toño,** a good, economic choice for classic Mexican fare like pozole, quesadillas, etc. There's often a line to get in.

Continue on Londres, passing calle Amberes (a center of youth-oriented gay life). You'll see the **Mercado de Artesanias Insurgentes**

Ángel de la Independencia

(enter at Londres 152 or 154—look up for the sign) on your left. It's rather claustrophobic, but known for good silver jewelry. Just across the street is the **Plaza del Ángel**, where you'll find many little antique stores, and a weekend flea market.

At Florencia, with its majestic palm trees, turn right. Straight ahead you will see the **Ángel de la Independencia**. Inaugurated in 1910, it is most iconic image of Mexico City, appearing on just about every tourist brochure. If you're here on Saturday morning, you can climb to the top for some impressive views.

Carefully crossing the Paseo de la Reforma, head toward the high-rise HSBC building to your left. Inside is a **grand mural** by Mexican artist/architect Juan O'Gorman (he did the famous mosaic murals at the UNAM Library and the studios of Frida and Diego in San Ángel). The security team in the lobby here can be suspicious—just play dumb.

Having crossed Reforma, you are now in **Colonia Cuauhtémoc**, a mostly residential area and home to the American Embassy (Reforma 305) and several big chain hotels. All of the high-rise grandeur of the colonia, including the city's tallest building, the **Torre Mayor**, and the stock exchange, is along Reforma. Behind that imposing wall of development you'll find a quiet residential neighborhood.

Walk along Rio Tiber (the same street as Florencia—it changes name after crossing Reforma). Go two short blocks and turn right on Rio Lerma. This is the social hub of the neighborhood, with many restaurants and cafés, and a small market (near Danubio) with a great display of flowers out front.

At the corner of Lerma and Rio Sena is a handsome art deco building by Ernesto Buenrostro, who designed some of the best homes in the Condesa.

Further on at Lerma 86 (across from the British Embassy) is **La Bella Lula**, where you'll find good Oaxacan food. There's a lovely row of old houses on this block.

Take note of the **Edificio Eureka** (Lerma 46B, near Amazonas), a classic art deco place that now houses a popular local eatery.

Just ahead on your left (Lerma 35) is the **Museo Casa de Carranza**, the 19th-century home where former Mexican President Venustiano Carranza lived for a while in 1919, shortly before his assassination. Most of the furnishings are original, and the house exudes the magical charm of time travel—well worth a visit, even if you're not a history buff.

Further along Lerma is the colonial style **Hotel Maria Cristina**, a comfy, old-fashioned place for anyone wanting to stay in a quiet area. Lerma ends just ahead at Plaza Carlos Finlay. Turn left and you'll see **Parque Sullivan** in front of you. On Sundays the park is filled with local artists selling their work.

Directly across the park is the **Museo Experimental El Eco**, a small art space designed in the 1950's by noted Mexican artist Mathias Goeritz. This street (James Sullivan) marks the limit of Colonia Cuauhtémoc and the beginning of Colonia San Rafael.

At the end of the park (going right, near Insurgentes) is the **Monumento de la Madre**. Completed in 1949, this rather grim, imposing homage to motherhood is unlikely to recall happy moments from childhood.

Walk along James Sullivan toward Insurgentes (you'll see a Metrobús stop), cross the street and walk down Calle Madrid (there's a big sign for SEPS restaurant). You have just crossed over into **Colonia Tabacalera**. At Madrid 3 is one of the few old houses left in this area, and at the end of the street on your right, is the Telmex building, a good example of art deco design with nice iron work and stone panels of old telephones over the doorways.

Monumento de la Madre

Turn left here (the sign says Madrid, but the name changes to Vallarta just across the street). Just as you pass the massive CTM building (labor union) on your right you come to the **Monumento de la Revolución**, which has great views from its mirador (opens at noon.)

The tour ends here, or continue with Walking Tour #6 (p. 86).

There is a taxi sitio in front of Calle Vallarta #1, a Metrobús stop on Insurgentes, and a metro stop three blocks away on Puente de Alvarado.

BOSQUE DE CHAPULTEPEC

The city's largest green area was a forest refuge even before the *conquistadores* arrived, and the first Spanish viceroy, Antonio de Mendoza, officially designated it a public park over 400 years ago. During the week, it is fairly quiet, but on weekends, families flock to the park and it takes on a carnival atmosphere. There are several good museums here and a well kept zoo. The park is open from 5am to 6pm every day except Monday. From April 1 through October it's open until 7pm. If you arrive by metro (Chapultepec stop on #1 line), follow the signs marked Bosque de Chapultepec or Castillo and cross over the pedestrian bridge into the park.

The main entrance to the park is on Reforma just opposite the **Torre Mayor**, Mexico's tallest building (use the underpass marked **Paseo de Peatones** from this side). Next to the big iron entrance gates is the **Torre Bicentenario**, a tall narrow tower that was designed to celebrate Mexico's 200 years of independence from Spain in 2010. Due to scandalous delays and cost overruns, it has become known to locals as a monument to corruption.

A pedestrian bridge takes you over the busy *periférico*, the city's traffic beltway. Huge white columns flank the park's entry, a monument to Los Niños Héroes, the young cadets who defended the hill against invading Americans in 1847.

To your left is the entrance road to the **Castillo de Chapultepec**, which you can see at the top of the hill—follow the signs for the **Museo Nacional de Historia**. This spot marks the "Halls of Montezuma" referred to in the Marines' Hymn. There's an impressive 360 degree view from the top—a 13-peso mini-train ride will get you up the hill if you don't feel like walking. Along the way, you'll pass by the **Museo del Caracol**, recommended only for die-hard historians who read Spanish.

The oldest parts of the castle date back to 1785, but its historical importance to Mexicans is as the final holdout in the American War of 1847, when six young cadets (the famous "Niños Héroes") wrapped themselves in the Mexican flag and jumped to their death rather than surrender to the Americans. There are streets and even a metro stop named after Los Niños Héroes.

In the 1860's the ill-fated Hapsburg Emperor Maximilian and his wife Carlotta remodeled the Castillo as their home, introducing elegant European furniture, gardens, and fabulous bathrooms. Maximilian was also responsible for the **Paseo de la Reforma,** which he created as a grand promenade, modeled on the Champs Elysees, between his home and the government offices on the Zócalo. President Porfirio Díaz lived here, too, but since 1940 it has been a museum. The building has two sections. The **Alcázar** contains the residential quarters, carefully restored in period style, with formal gardens—be sure to go upstairs. The other section is the **Museo Nacional de Historia**, with artwork and documents about Mexican history. Don't miss the impressive murals

Castillo de Chapultepec

by Siqueiros, Orozco, and my favorite, Juan O'Gorman (in Salas 6 and 11), three important artists of the muralist movement of the 1920's through the 1940's.

Back down the hill is the **Museo de Arte Moderno** (you'll see the back entrance - the main entrance is on Reforma). There is an important permanent collection of 20th century Mexican paintings and sculpture here, as well as temporary exhibits. Frida Kahlo's famous *Las dos Fridas* is part of this collection (but often out on loan).

The main path through the park (you'll see lots of vendors) will take you to the oddly green lake, where you can rent a boat if you like. From here you can follow signs to the zoo and the **Museo de Antropología** (see below).

As you exit the park facing the Museo de Antropología, check out the metal fences along Reforma. They are used for interesting outdoor photo exhibitions that change every few months. You can get a bus or taxi on Reforma heading to the Centro. There's also a taxi sitio in front of the museum, but it's pricey.

Entrance to the Museo Rufino Tamayo.

A short walk from the Museo de Antropología is the **Museo Rufino Tamayo** (*www.museotamayo.org*), housed in another beautiful building, which was awarded the 1981 National Art Prize. Tamayo, one of Mexico's most important 20th-century artists, donated a large collection of works by many artists to the museum, but you don't often see much of his own work there. Temporary exhibits change every few months. There's a good gift shop and a lovely restaurant/café with a view of the park.

You can walk to nearby Colonia Condesa after visiting the park: return to Metro Chapultepec. Use the pedestrian underpass and take the exit marked Calz. de Tacubaya—don't go through the turnstile. You'll be near the end of Avenida Veracruz.

Food and drink in the park

There are lots of small eateries within the park, but I can't say I've been too impressed with any of them. The Museo de Antropología has a decent restaurant on the lower level. For better food options head to nearby Colonia Condesa or Polanco *(see FOOD section)*.

MUSEO NACIONAL DE ANTROPOLOGÍA

(Paseo de la Reforma in Parque Chapultepec, www.mna.inah.gob.mx)

This is one of the great museums of the world, with the most impressive collection of pre-Hispanic art anywhere. Don't miss it! The building, designed by Pedro Ramírez Vásquez and inaugurated in 1964, is a modern interpretation of a pre-Hispanic town center, with all its treasures on display. Spatial proportions echo the peaceful vastness of Teotihuacán, decorative screens on the upper floor are updated versions of bas-reliefs from Mayan temples, a pond filled with papyrus and turtles in the patio recalls the lakes and marshes the Aztecs first encountered here. A stately waterfall/fountain supports the dramatically cantilevered roof. All rooms open toward this central patio in classic Mexican style, but also have access to leafy garden areas behind each gallery.

The collection is organized roughly in chronological and geographical order, starting on the right side. The first rooms trace early primitive culture. Be sure to walk through the **Sala Preclásico** to the back garden and see a recreation of a *troje*, the typical wooden house of Michoacán. The **Sala Teotihuacán** gives you a good idea of what awaits at the actual ruins, just outside the city limits.

There is too much here to take in during a single visit, so don't try. If your time is limited, I recommend you walk straight through the open patio to the far end and enter the **Sala Mexica**, whose sculptures and artifacts illuminate Aztec culture. It is the biggest and most important part of the museum's collection. The famous 'Aztec Calendar' (which is not a calendar after all) is here along with much surprising sculpture and jewelry, and interesting scale models of the city in Aztec times.

Culturas de Oaxaca features beautiful polychrome pottery and some fascinating cartoon-like codices (long narrative scrolls).

Culturas de la Costa del Golfo highlights include the mammoth Olmec heads, among the oldest and most impressive of pre-Hispanic artifacts. Figurative sculptures with laughing faces offer a surprising glimpse of humor. The Mayan people, along with the Aztecs, produced the most refined and complex art and architecture in Mexico. In the Sala Maya, don't miss the carved stelae from Yáxchilan and the reproduction of a Mayan temple in the back garden.

Culturas de Occidente displays objects from Mexico's early western cultures, which predate the Aztecs by many centuries. Curious flattened figures from Nayarit and charming animal sculptures from Colima are standouts here, as are the many unusually shaped pots.

Upstairs are exhibitions about the indigenous population. Mexico has more than 56 different ethnic groups.

Sala Teotihuacá

Almost 2 million people still speak Nahuatl and one million speak Maya. Typical houses, dress, items for daily and ritual use, and handicrafts are displayed. What makes it more interesting is realizing that most of what you see here is still found in many parts of rural Mexico, and one can occasionally overhear Nahuatl being spoken, even here in the city (lots of soft shhh sounds).

As you exit the museum, listen for the sounds of flute and drum. If you are lucky, you'll catch the **Voladores de Papantla** performing across from the museum in the park. Four men, whose feet are lashed to ropes on a 75-foot pole, slowly revolve downward, as a fifth man dances and plays music on a small plat-

form at the top, with no rope attached. What you see is an offering to the fertility god Xipe Totec, a ritual of the Totonac people from the state of Veracruz, who have been doing it for centuries. It's a bit of a tourist show—they ask for a "donation"—but gripping nonetheless.

A tourist information kiosk and a Taxi de Turismo stand (expensive—check fares first) are in front of the museum on Reforma. The less expensive taxi sitio is a 5-minute walk along Reforma at Auditorio Nacional. There are frequent buses in both directions. Those marked Metro Hidalgo or Reforma/La Villa will take you to the western end of the Alameda. Less frequent ones go all the way to the Zócalo.

THE BEST PRE-HISPANIC ART COLLECTIONS IN MEXICO CITY

No place in the world has the concentration of high quality pre-Hispanic art that you'll find in Mexico City. You can't claim to understand Mexico without seeing some of this art. Here are the top places to see it:

- Museo de Antropología (p. 104)
- Museo del Templo Mayor (p. 60)
- Anahuacalli (p. 145)
- Museo Dolores Olmedo (p. 152)
- Colección Stavenhagen, Tlatelolco (p. 156)
- Museo Soumaya (p. 137)

THE CONTEMPORARY ART SCENE

Museo Jumex

Much has been written about the burgeoning contemporary art scene in Mexico, but it can sometimes be frustratingly hard to find. Art galleries are scattered around the city, and there is no comprehensive gallery guide. Check *TimeOut* and *Tiempo Libre* magazines for current listings.

Several annual **international art fairs** have helped raise the ante. The dates vary (usually late winter/early spring), so check the websites:

www.zonamaco.com

www.material-fair.com

www.affordableartfair.com/mexicocity

www.galleryweekendmexico.com

The **Corredor Cultural Condesa Roma** occurs twice a year and features local galleries. Consult website for dates:
www.ccromacondesa.mx

Museo Jumex in Polanco, inaugurated in late 2013, is now the city's top contemporary art museum. *www.fundacionjumex.org*

The Museo del Chopo offers temporary exhibits, often with an edge, and they have a big LGBT art show in June. *www.chopo.unam.mx*

MUAC (Museo Universitario Arte Contemporaneo) offers changing exhibits of international contemporarty art. *www.muac.unam.mx*

Commercial galleries are concentrated in a few neighborhoods, but are spread out within these areas. Galleries come and go, and some have no set hours. Here are a few suggestions of established galleries.

Colonia Roma
OMR, *www.galeriaomr.com*
Arróniz, *www.arroniz-arte.com*
Galería Metropolitana, *www.galeriametropolitana.mx*
Machete, *www.macheteart.com*

San Miguel Chapultepec
Kurimanzutto, *www.kurimanzutto.com*
Labor, *www.labor.org.mx*
Galeria Nina Menocal, *www.ninamenocal.com*
Myto, *www.mytogallery.com*

San Rafael
Yautepec, *www.yau.com.mx*
Hilario Galguera, *www.galeriahilariogalguera.com*
On Facebook: *Asociación de Galerías de Arte de San Rafael*

Polanco
Galería López Quiroga, *www.lopezquiroga.com*
Patricia Conde, *www.patriciacondegaleria.com*
Galería Alfredo Ginocchi, *www.ginocchiogaleria.com*

VISIT A TRADITIONAL MEXICAN MARKET

If you have already been to the Museo de Antropología, you may have seen the diorama recreating an Aztec market. You can visit the real thing today and see how little has changed in 500 years. I include this in my book less as a shopping experience (although you are unlikely to leave empty-handed), than as a cultural one. More than just a place to buy groceries, market shopping is part of a traditional way of life that is gradually changing as more American-style supermarkets appear on the scene—so go while you can. Many individual vendors, usually all of a family, join together at these markets, which creates an old-fashioned village ambience.

Mexicans have a particular knack for displaying fruits and vegetables, arranging avocados in gravity-defying piles, cutting pink grapefruits to look like origami, splaying a ripe pomegranate into glistening segments. Meat and fish vendors might make many foreign visitors queasy—no plastic wrap and Styrofoam separate you from the reality of the dead animal. Although today's markets offer sneakers, t-shirts and mountains of junk made in China, you can still find traditional handicrafts such as pottery and baskets for sale.

At holiday times, especially Easter, Day of the Dead and Christmas, markets are filled with traditional foods and decorations.

Some great prepared food is found inside and around markets. You'll usually find stands selling tamales and tlacoyos outside market buildings, and inside there is usually a group of *comedores* (small eateries) serving inexpensive traditional Mexican fare.

Close your eyes and listen to the sounds in the market, too. *Pregones* are the traditional calls that vendors cry out urging one to buy. *¿Qué va a llevar?* (literally "What are you going to carry away?") or *¿Qué le damos, marchanta?* ("What can we give you, customer?") are among the many phrases that will be repeated often as you pass by. You do not need to respond to every call.

Every neighborhood in Mexico City has its market, but a few are standouts: **The Mercado Jamaica** and **La Merced**, my two favorites, are described below. Other important markets are in **Coyoacán**, **Xochimilco**, the **Mercado Medellín** in Colonia Roma, and the **Mercado San Juan** in the Centro.

TIANGUIS, MERCADOS SOBRE RUEDAS

The Nahuatl word *tianguis* means an open air market that is traditionally held on certain days; these once-a-week neighborhood street markets have been a fixture of Mexico City life since Aztec times. Rooted in pre-automobile society, the store comes to you, usually once a week in most residential areas. Vendors set up tarp-covered stalls in the street, supplying all your basic household needs. Neighbors come to shop and eat in an atmosphere of festive bustling, suddenly turning the city into a village. They are sometimes referred to as *mercado sobre ruedas*, markets on wheels. There are especially attractive and clean tianguis in the Condesa on Tuesdays and Fridays and Polanco on Saturday.

Mercado Jamaica (Jamaica is pronounced "ha-MY-ka") is located at the corner of Avenida Morelos and Congreso de la Unión, about a mile south of the Zócalo. This is my favorite market in Mexico City, the most colorful and picturesque of them all. As well as a produce market, this is the city's wholesale flower market; I come here every few weeks to stock up on flowers. Any taxi driver will know it, but it's an easy place to reach by metro—the Jamaica stop is on the #9 train.

Look up to see the big *Mi Mercado* sign (all Mexico City markets have this same sign) at the corner of the market building and start there. The main building is a big concrete and tin bulk painted turquoise and green. The attractions here are a good selection of basketry at one end, some elaborate fruit baskets, a beauty parlor run by transvestites, and stands selling tepache, a traditional drink of slightly fermented pineapple juice, something like cider. But the most interesting parts of the market lie beyond this in several open-sided buildings. There is a stall offering rare tropical fruits, one with many kinds of eggs, another with different kinds of mole in paste form, and several displays of household items made of day-glo plastic. Look up to see papier maché piñatas and all kinds of market bags for sale—they last forever and make good gifts. This market is open, spacious, and rarely crowded, making it much easier to maneuver than most.

As you wander further on you will discover the main **flower market** of Mexico City, the real highlight of this place. Row after row of vendors selling mountains of seasonal flowers at extremely low prices, open 24 hours a day, 365 days a year. It always dazzles, with colors and scents vibrating in hedonistic excess. Around Valentine's Day and Mothers' Day, roses of every color fill the aisles up to your shoulders; truckloads of golden marigolds and purple-red coxcombs arrive for Day of the Dead. Armfuls of pure white calla lilies (famously painted by Diego Rivera) are on sale, as are black gladiolas and daisies dyed sky blue. There are flowers for every occasion between birth and death. Over-

the-top arrangements might incorporate fruit, plastic dolls, and even live goldfish, with vivid color combinations you would not find anywhere but Mexico.

There are vendors selling inexpensive vases, too, so you can buy flowers for your hotel room, or to bring to a friend.

This market is famous for its huaraches—not the kind you wear, the kind you eat. Masa (the corn dough used to make tortillas) is formed into long ovals—more or less the shape of a shoe, hence the name. Cooked on a griddle and topped with meat, cheese, or eggs, you will see them being aggressively sold in the covered market building.

There is a taxi sitio behind the flower market—just ask if you don't see it.

La Merced The mother of all markets, this massive conglomeration of buildings covering several acres has been an active market area since the 17th century. As late as the early 20th century the area was criss-crossed by canals and goods were delivered in canoes. The commercial frenzy extends for blocks and blocks toward the Zócalo with wholesale merchants selling just about anything you can think of. (see Walking Tour #4, p. 74).

The area lies 1km southeast of the Zócalo. Just ask any taxi driver to take you to La Merced, or better yet, ride the metro. Take the #1 train to the La Merced stop. If you exit at the front end of the train, you will be right in the middle of the main market building. It's the best way to arrive.

Exploring in any direction, you will find piles of banana leaves and corn husks for making tamales, walls of dried chilies, mountains of garlic, large cylinders of stacked nopal cactus paddles, wild mushrooms, exotic fruits, and vegetables, herbs, spices, mole—just about anything edible produced in Mexico.

Near the metro exit is a wide staircase leading to a lower level (the sign says *Desnivel*—ask if you don't see it) where you will find dry goods including baskets, metalwork and traditional Mexican costumes for children. Outside this huge main building are several smaller buildings, each with a different specialty. The ones for sweets, fake flowers, and kitchenware are fun for the staggering quantity of goods on display.

La Merced can be one of the most hectic places in the city, but if you move in a relaxed way, it can be a lot of fun. If you already feel over-whelmed by Mexico City, however, this market is not for you. It is best visited between 9 and noon; it can get uncomfortably crowded after that, especially on weekends.

Along the west side of the main building are many food stalls, a great place to try some quesadillas of flor de calabaza or huitlacoche.

For a moment of tranquility, visit the nearby **Templo de San Tomás la Palma**, between the candy market and the artificial flowers—ask any vendor for directions.

If you still have some steam left, you might want to visit the **Mercado Sonora,** a few blocks from La Merced, (crossing Fray Servando at the pedestrian overpass.) It is commonly known as the witches' market. In the first few aisles on the left (Pasillo 8) vendors sell herbs, folk medicines, candles, voodoo dolls, amulets, and all sorts of things for casting spells to get rich or fall in love.

A few aisles over you can find some good traditional pottery (mixed in with lots of hideous new things) and an unappealing section of caged animals.

COLONIAS AND BARRIOS

The words colonia and barrio are often used interchangeably, but both refer to a neighborhood, a self-contained area with its own distinct characteristics. Although Mexico is a city with more than 20 million inhabitants, it's really made up of lots of smaller neighborhoods all linked together. There are 16 delegaciones (like New York's boroughs) and within them many, many colonias. To get a true feeling of the city, spend time in one of these areas to see how people live. Local markets, shops and restaurants, and especially active street life (vendors, musicians, street sweepers) will tell you much more than any museum about what it means to live in Mexico City.

COLONIA CONDESA

Colonia Condesa, a residential area inaugurated in 1925, is one of the loveliest parts of Mexico City. It has two parks, many tree-lined streets, sleek modern apartment buildings, lots of outdoor cafés, trendy restaurants, and good bookstores. Its wealth of art deco architecture rivals Miami. It attracts artists, actors, writers, yuppies, hipsters, and many foreigners. But it still retains a healthy dose of old-fashioned neighbourhood ambience, despite the arrival of Starbucks, cupcake stores and high rents.

Condesa is the perfect place to visit when the city starts to feel too much to handle, and it's especially tranquil on Sundays and holidays. If you visit on a Tuesday or Friday, you can see the colorful weekly tianguis.

The best way to experience the Condesa is on foot or bicycle. The four connected walking tours below will take you through the prettiest and liveliest parts of the colonia. The urban plan here is complicated—lots of circles, spokes and non-parallel streets. The first two walks are no-brainers, as there are no turns—you'll just walk along two large oval streets, returning where you began.

WALKING TOUR #9:
Around Parque México

📣 **Start the tour on Avenida Michoacán at Parque México** where you'll see a statue of a naked woman holding two jugs with water spilling into the fountain. This emblematic image of La Condesa adorns the entrance to the **Foro Lindbergh**, the large open space in front of you that is used for concerts and other public events on weekends. It's named for Charles Lindbergh as its inauguration coincided with his transatlantic crossing of 1927. The park is filled with huge old banana trees, a geyser-like fountain, a duck pond, and lots of space for the many fancy dogs that live nearby. It's a lovely place to stroll or relax on one of the old covered benches. This is the heart of Colonia Condesa.

"Fuente de los Cántaros" fountain in Parque México.

The street surrounding the park is Avenida México. Start at the corner of Michoacán and Avenida México—in front of the taxi stand—and walk clockwise around the park. The big white building that looks like an art deco ocean liner at the corner is a 1934 work of Francisco Serrano, an architect who designed some of the best buildings in Condesa—there'll be more of his work along the way. Notice the charming neo-colonial style houses at #63 and #59, and the art deco Edificio Roxy (#33) with its fabulous penthouse. Peek into the lobby at #27 to see the staircase.

Fountain in Parque México.

The next corner, Av. Sonora, marks the official entry to the park with a small bust of José de San Martín, the Argentine freedom fighter after whom the park is named (nobody uses that name, however— around here, it's known to all as Parque México).

Continue on Avenida México away from the park (toward the pharmacy). A block ahead is **Plaza Popocatépetl**, a round leafy plaza with a fountain and benches. Walking around the plaza you'll see Origines Orgánicos, where locals go for healthy food, and the beautifully restored art deco Edificio Lux (#36). Take a short detour to Celaya 25 to the home of the American Legion—the original interior details are impressive, and there's a good English-language bookstore upstairs.

Fountain at Plaza Popcatépetl.

Complete the loop around Plaza Popocatépetl and continue along Avenida México, (there's a big blue house on the corner). At #187 you'll see the grand staircase of **Edifico Basurto**, another Serrano building of the 1940's, and across the street (#188), the **Edificio Tehuacán**, another art deco gem that's been modernized—note the bas-relief panels above (it is now a boutique hotel and restaurant).

Continue on Avenida México, crossing the wide intersection at Sonora back toward the park. The rather unassuming glass box at #175 is where former Mexico City mayor (and future presidential hopeful) Marcelo Ebrard lived during his tenure. The classy **Edificio San Martin** (#167) is one of the most desirable addresses on the park; it has been meticulously restored to its deco splendor.

Edificio Tehuacán, Col. Condesa, now a hotel.

Two early buildings by **Luis Barragán** (check the name plaque) are located at #143 and #141. At #123 is another Serrano building, somewhat forlorn— but that front door! The tortas at the small shop next door are the best in the area.

As you continue around the park on Avenida México, you'll return to Michoacán, where we began.

The following tour continues from here.

Edificio San Martín, on Avenida México, Col. Condesa.

WALKING TOUR #10:

Avenida Amsterdam

☛ **From the Parque México taxi sitio (see tour #9), walk along Michoacán** (following the direction of traffic) and go one block to Avenida Amsterdam. There's a Superama supermarket at the corner. Mornings and evenings a vendor sells an interesting variety of tamales out front.

Turn right on Amsterdam and walk down the *camellón*, the green walkway that divides the street. Avenida Amsterdam is a giant oval, what's left of a 19th century racetrack that was here before the area was subdivided for housing in the 1920's.

At #110 is yet another house by Serrano, a bit neglected. At Calle Parras, to your left, you'll find a row of small restaurants, where locals go for an inexpensive comida corrida. Take a look upstairs in the restaurant at #67 to appreciate how these old houses might have looked.

Continue along the curve of Amsterdam, crossing Sonora. At the corner of Cacajuamilpa is my vote for one of the ugliest buildings around. Just past that, on your right, is **La Bodega,** a popular nightspot featuring live Cuban music and an upstairs cabaret. The ambience feels like old Greenwich Village and the Mexican food is quite good.

At #317 is Qi, the upscale gym where you can go for a spa treatment or a workout. Try the merengues at the Pastelería Gran Via, in the Edificio Teresa (#288)—one of my favorite desserts in all of Mexico.

Look into the lobby at #285 at the corner of Sonora, another beautifully maintained early deco building by Francisco Serrano.

Continue along the camellón of Avenida Amsterdam. The mysterious and incongruous geodesic domed structure at #270 is the work of the late Juan José Díaz Infante, architect of the Mexican stock exchange. The restaurant Matisse at #260 is a local landmark—the food is unexceptional, although desserts are good; the interior, especially

Camellón of Avenida Amsterdam.

upstairs, is worth a look. Down the block, peek into the lobbies of #252 and #248 (those floor tiles!). Look up at #247 at the corner of Michoacán to see another possible winner in the 'ugly building' contest—the mix is quintessential Mexico City.

Continue on Amsterdam to **Plaza Iztaccíhuatl** (by now you should have noticed the Nahuatl inspired names here, even if you can't pronounce them), one of the charming 'interruptions' of the grand oval of Amsterdam. At Amsterdam #205 is another Serrano building displaying impressive metal work. The restaurant MeroToro, just next door, is one of the city's most acclaimed dining spots.

Walk around **Plaza Citlaltepetl**, with its minimalist fountain, and continue along the camellón of Amsterdam. At the next corner, Ozulama, you'll see one of the few examples of neo-gothic architecture around, and, across the street, a purveyor of fine chocolates, Tout Chocolat.

*You'll see the Superama again at the next corner of Michoacán—turn right to reach the taxi stand, or **go left to continue on Walking Tour #11.***

WALKING TOUR #11:
Commerce and Nightlife

☞ **This tour starts where the last one ends**—at the corner of Amsterdam and Sonora, in front of the Superama.

Follow Avenida Michoacán in the direction of traffic. At #54 in the Edifico Michoacán is the **Taquería El Greco**, an old stand-by for 'tacos árabes', the culinary grandfather of the more common tacos al pastor.

Continuing on Michoacán, cross the wide avenue, Nuevo León. Near the far corner, **Xel-Ha** is a popular cantina serving Yucatecan food—it's a favorite gathering place for foreign journalists.

Walk a block further on Michoacán to the wide intersection of Tamaulipas. The Condesa market will be straight ahead of you. It's not one of the city's best markets, but it's good to see a bit of old-style Mexico City in this otherwise trendy neighborhood. There's a stop for the Turibus at this corner.

At the next corner (Michoacán and Atlixco) you're in the commercial hub of Condesa, a 'downtown' that consists mostly of restaurants. It's one of the most interesting and attractive of the many playgrounds where privileged youth of Mexico go out for a good time. There are many pleasant restaurants here, although this isn't usually where you'll find the best food.

As you continue on Michoacán, you'll see familiar signs of gentrification —venues for upscale pizza, frozen yogurt, Krispy Kreme donuts. When you reach Cuautla (Condesa 439 Bar), make a 360-degree left turn on to Campeche, a lovely residential street graced with tall palm trees. Near Atlixco (#393) notice the hand-painted signs in the barbershop, the tailor and the dry cleaner shops—remnants of the Condesa of yesteryear.

At the far right corner of Campeche at Tamaulipas is **El Tizoncito**, one of Mexico's most famous taquerías—they claim that tacos al pastor

Av. Vicente Suárez looking east from Av. Michoacán and Calle Atlixco.

originated here. In any case, it's a great place to try them—their salsas are excellent. (If it's full, there's a branch two blocks further along Campeche at Cholula.)

From Campeche, turn right on Tamaulipas. At Alfonso Reyes is the landmark Nevería Roxy, an ice cream store (so-so ice cream) and one of the few Catholic churches in the area, Santa Rosa.

There's a taxi sitio just across from the Roxy. The nearest metro stop is Patriotismo on the #9 line.

The **Centro Cultural Bella Época**, where the next tour starts, is just down the block at the corner of Tamaulipas and Benjamin Hill.

WALKING TOUR #12:
From Condesa to Roma under the trees

This tour takes you along tree-covered camellones through two of the nicest residential neighborhoods in the city.

☞ **Start in Condesa at the Centro Cultural Bella Época** (Benjamin Hill at Tamaulipas), a good bookstore with a small cinema and popular café. Follow Tamulipas (toward the news-stand) one block to Alfonso Reyes and turn left. The Church of Santa Rosa (1943) on the corner has a cool interior with lots of golden filigree decoration. The quiet, leafy side streets here are home to some of Condesa's most desirable real estate.

Continue along Alfonso Reyes and turn right when you reach Mazatlán, a grand avenue with some magnificent architecture, such as the purple house at #157 and the California style house at #102.

Further along Mazatlán, near Montes de Oca you'll find the Nevería Roxy, an old fashioned ice-cream shop—style trumps flavor here, unfortunately, and The Green Corner, a popular organic food shop and café. Note the grand portal at Mazatlán 73, the large apartment complex at #71-63 and the lovely arched doorway just across the street. There's a cluster of modernist style houses from #61 to #55, and a defiant little cottage squeezed into #34.

When you reach Calle Juan de la Barrera, you'll see a block-long greenish building on the left. This is the famous **Edifico Condesa**, sometimes referred to as Mexico's Peyton Place due to gossip about its famous residents over the past decades.

If you are here on a Tuesday, be sure to go behind the building (Calle Pachuca) to visit one of the city's best weekly **tianguis**. There are great street food options here.

Cross the big intersection on Mazatlán (the Pemex gas station is on your right), past the large cactus planter, and continue on the camellón of Calle Durango (which is essentially an extension of Mazatlán with a slight right turn). You have just left Colonia Condesa and entered Colonia Roma Norte.

At Durango 34 is one of the best examples of art deco design in the area, and at #315, largely hidden by trees, one of the few remaining mansions, now used as offices. Passing Sevilla, you'll see a branch of Palacio de Hierro, Mexico's major department store, on your right (clean bathrooms here). Their ad campaign 'Soy totalmente Palacio', which pokes fun at Mexico City's upper class, has become a classic of chilango humor. The street becomes a bit more commercial here— newer, higher glass boxes dominate. Just off Durango (Valladolid 55B) Julio de la Torre has stocked his store with well-chosen 20th century furniture and accessories.

A block ahead on Durango is the **Glorieta de las Cibeles**, a round plaza with a copy of Madrid's famous statue in the middle. In recent years, this plaza has made a comeback, luring diners and drinkers to its attractive outdoor spaces. If you are here on a Wednesday or Friday, stroll through the tianguis on Calle Oro, just off the plaza. There are some great street food stalls in the first aisle.

(A few blocks off the plaza the Galería Metropolitana (Medellín 28) offers interesting art exhibitions. *www.galeriametropolitana.mx*)

This tour ends here.

You can ask for a cab at any of the local restaurants. Walking north (across the plaza from where you entered) on Calle Oaxaca, with its majestic palm trees, will take you to Metro Insurgentes. There is a

Turibús stop on the plaza in front of #9, and a Metrobús stop a block away at Durango and Insurgentes.

THE TIANGUIS IN LA CONDESA

Most neighborhoods in Mexico City have a weekly street market known by the Aztec name *tianguis*. In Condesa, the Tuesday and Friday tianguis may remind you of street markets in Paris, without the cheese and the attitude. The produce is of high quality and is beautifully displayed; there are some good cooked food stalls, too.

The Tuesday tianguis is located on Calle Pachuca between Veracruz and Juan de la Barrera, not far from the Chapultepec metro station. Try the *tacos de mixiote* (shredded pork in a spicy red sauce) and *empanadas de camarón* (fried pastries with shrimp, avocado, onion, and cilantro). There are good quesadilla and tlacoyo vendors, too. My favorite tamales are here: Doña Marta sells excellent *tamales de mole* and *tamales oaxaqueños* (in a banana leaf) at the corner of Pachuca and Veracruz—she usually sells out by 11am. There is a taxi sitio two blocks from the market at the corner of Augustin Melgar and José Vasconcelos

The smaller Friday tianguis is at the corner of Nuevo León and Campeche. There's an old-fashioned neighborhood feel here, with baskets and pottery being sold along with fruits and vegetables, meat and fish. The prepared food stalls are great. You'll find superior *tacos de cecina adobada* (pounded pork with chile) that you can wash down with *tepache* (a lightly fermented drink made from pineapple juice), and the homemade *torta de elote* (sweet corn cake) is dense and satisfying. You will also see people lining up for fresh blue corn quesadillas and tlacoyos. The taxi sitio in Parque México is a few blocks away.

COLONIA ROMA

I rented my first apartment in Mexico City in 1998 in Colonia Roma, before it became the hotspot it is today. The 2-bedroom 1950's-era apartment was cheap enough to overlook the ugly block with its earthquake damaged buildings and garbage strewn *vecindades*. How things have changed!

Built during the last years of the dictatorship of Porfirio Díaz, Colonia Roma expressed the French influence Díaz promoted all over the country. It was his attempt to make Mexico look like a world-class city (the ornate cast-iron kiosks found in the main squares of many Mexican towns date from this era). Roma was the first fully planned subdivision, with underground electric cables, running water, and even a trolley line. It was home to famous politicians, actors, writers and bullfighters. For the first few decades of the 20th century, it was *the* place to live. Then, as the city expanded to the west and huge mansions became white elephants, the area went into a decades long decline, only recently returning to life.

The original architecture features stone arches, balustrades, cornices, and garlands, plus ornate ironwork and the occasional use of glazed tiles. Several small plazas with fountains and classical statuary, and a tree-shaded walkway down its main drag, Álvaro Obregón, added to the charm. It was designed as a place for strolling, stopping for a café, or to

get your shoes shined before heading home. Many of the old buildings are gone, replaced by a hodgepodge of charmless apartment buildings, but enough remains to give Colonia Roma its distinctive charm. And you still find some of the old world touches like street sweepers using handmade twig brooms, a guy pushing a wheelbarrow full of traditional candies, or an itinerant shoelace vendor. You can sense the Mexico City of another, more graceful, era, one that moved to the pace of horse and carriage.

From the beginning Roma was a mixed neighborhood, a sociological experiment in egalitarianism. Grand mansions sat next to apartment buildings and single-family houses of various economic levels ranging from middle to upper class. In the 1930's the money began to move west to newer colonias, like Condesa and Polanco, and decay set in. Many houses of the Porfiriato period were torn down and replaced with more utilitarian buildings, often of surprising ugliness. Mansions became offices and schools. The earthquake of 1985 severely damaged the area, leaving it neglected and unloved.

But over the past decade or so, Roma has experienced a boom, as a new generation has begun to polish its faded glory. Restaurants, cool cafés, bookstores, boutiques, art galleries, and organic food stores are sprouting like whiskers on an adolescent's chin. Even the garbage collectors add to the eclectic mix—one truck I passed was blaring Roy Orbison's 'Pretty Woman.'

Roma is a great area to stay in: its location provides easy access to most of the major tourist sites in the city. It's also a nice place just to hang out, walk around, and soak up the ambience of one of the city's most eclectic and attractive neighborhoods.

Orientation: *The intersection of Orizaba and Álvaro Obregón, and the adjacent side streets, is the area's hub where most of commerce is clustered. There are two small parks along Orizaba, Plaza Río de Janiero, with its reproduction of Michaelangelo's David, and Plaza Luis Cabrera, which now sports its own Starbucks. The streets Colima, Tabasco, Durango, and Jalapa are the most attractive.*

WALKING TOUR #13:
COLONIA ROMA, History with Hipsters

☛ **Begin your tour at the corner of Insurgentes and Álvaro Obregón**—take a taxi, or there's a Metrobús stop 'Álvaro Obregón'.

Walk east on Álvaro Obregón (look for a cluster of torta and taco stands). The first cross street will be Monterrey. At this corner is **Delirio**, a popular place for breakfast or lunch (closed Mondays). Their home-brand marmalades and chili salsas make great gifts.

Straight ahead on Álvaro Obregón at #186 is **Trouvé**, a store specializing in mid-century modern furniture and accessories.

Turn left at Tonalá, crossing Álvaro Obregón. On the far right corner is a lovely old mansion, which now houses the offices of the state of Quintana Roo.

Continue on Tonalá, past Tabasco (where you can see the typical angled corners of the old buildings) to Colima. This is one the best-preserved spots in La Roma—all four corner buildings are original. There's some remarkable ironwork at #52, and across the street (#51) you'll find **MUCA Roma** (Museo Universitaria de Ciencias y Arte), a small museum with changing shows, usually of a fairly cerebral nature. Admission is free. The roof terrace here is worth a look.

Turn right on Colima. The houses between #236 and #226 are among the most attractive in the area. The street has several shops and a good bakery. The next corner, Jalapa, is one of the ugliest around—three out of four original buildings are gone, and the fourth is in grim condition. But that's Colonia Roma for you.

Continue straight on Colima, past the Salón de la Plástica Mexicana (#196), a government sponsored art gallery, where the changing shows vary greatly in quality—good luck. Just next-door is the **Centro Gallego**, a cultural center for Spaniards from Galicia in northern Spain. The building is one of the grandest old mansions in Roma—check out that staircase. The claustrophobic restaurant downstairs is popular with local businessmen.

Two art galleries, **Fifty24MX** (#184) and **Traeger + Pinto** (#179) are worth a stop, as is the café **La Panaderia**, stepchild of **Rosetta** (#166), the excellent Italian restaurant just down the street.

Crossing Orizaba, continue one more block more on Colima and turn left at Córdoba. At the corner is the quirky museum **MODO (Museo del Objeto del Objeto**, *www.elmodo.mx*), whose changing exhibits define culture through everyday objects. You might find something for the folks back home in their gift shop. Check out the 'love locks' linked to the fence in front—a new expression of Mexican folk art.

Continue along Córdoba to #69, the headquarters of **Artes de México**, the much-admired magazine of Mexican art and culture. The gate is often locked, but just ring and they'll let you in. There's a small gift shop in the back. Try to peek upstairs where the offices are—the original architectural details of this former home are lovely.

Continue to the end of the block and turn left on Durango. At #87 you'll find the San Cristóbal antiques store, which often looks closed—just ring the bell. This place has the feel of grandma's attic, with some choice items (not cheap) of Mexican artesanías.

Straight ahead is **Plaza Río de Janeiro**, with its fountain splashing and a reproduction of Michelangelo's David, sans fig leaf. The building on the right corner houses the **Galería OMR**, one of the city's most prestigious, and on the left is an old apartment building known

as Las Brujas (The Witches), for the witch's hat roof of the tower.

Directly across the park from OMR is **Arróniz Arte Contemporáneo**, another of Roma's top art galleries. At the far left corner of the park (#65) is one of the prettiest buildings in Roma, adorned with fruit garlands carved in stone and intricate ironwork.

Turn left toward Orizaba (the way David's butt faces). At the corner of Tabasco on the right is the chic Hotel Brick, set in an old mansion. (Closed at the time of writing)

One block further is the intersection of Orizaba and Álvaro Obregón, the heart of Colonia Roma. On the right is the **Edificio Balmori**, and elegant apartment building from 1922, which now has several

trendy shops on its ground floor, including the cozy tea shop Caravansarai. On the left is **Casa Lamm**, a former mansion transformed into a cultural center, with a bookstore, galleries, art library, café, and upscale restaurant. Be sure to go upstairs to see the original rooms with their elaborate molding and woodwork. If you get a chance to attend one of their art openings, it's a great people-watching opportunity (check out the shoes on the upper-class crowd!).

Continue straight along Orizaba, passing the retro-style Bella Italia ice cream shop (décor trumps flavor however), and **Café d'Carlo**, serving some of the best coffee around. The next block, past Calle Chihuahua, is flanked by two more former mansions, now used as schools.

Directly in front of you is **Plaza Luis Cabrera**, where the beat poets used to hang out in the 1950's—now there's a Starbucks. Be sure to check out the elegant old home at #9 with its wrap-around portal.

Turn left on Zacatecas, noticing the ornate decoration on #94 (another school). At the next corner (Cordoba) is one of the disturbingly ugly buildings of Roma, a big orange concrete hulk. Diagonally across from that is one of the last remaining *tortillerías* in Roma, where you can see fresh tortillas being cranked out—or buy 5 pesos worth for a snack.

Further along Zacatecas at #59 is the **Pozolería Tizka**, which has delicious green pozole—one of my all-time favorite meals in the city. I lived upstairs from this place for five years and ate here often.

Turn left when you reach Merida. On the next corner (Guanajuato) on the right is an old art nouveau building which is currently being remodeled, little by little. When I first lived here, much of Roma looked like this.

Detour—(The best example of art nouveau architecture is down the block at Chihuahua 78).

Two blocks ahead is Álvaro Obregón—turn left here. Walk down the camellón in the middle of the street. It's especially nice in the late afternoon when the setting sun streaks through the trees. This will take you back to Insurgentes where this tour began. Along the way, on your right between Orizaba and Jalapa, is the **Pasaje El Parian**, a little architectural fantasy. It's one of the earliest 'shopping malls' in the city, now filled with hip stores.

There's a taxi sitio in front of Casa Lamm, near Calle Orizaba.

OTHER PLACES OF INTEREST IN COLONIA ROMA

Mercado Medellín (Coahuila between Medellín and Monterrey) is one of the city's top food markets. It is home to several stands selling Central, South Ameriacan and Carribean products, and has many good places to eat within and around it.

The Mercado Roma (225 Querétaro, between Medellin and Monterrey) is the newest addition to the area, inaugurated in 2014. It is a cool, upscale gourmet market for shopping and eating, similar to New York's Chelsea Market, but distinctly Mexican.

Monterrey 122 (near Chihuahua) In 1951 Beat Generation guru William Burroughs killed his wife Joan Vollmer here while trying to shoot an apple off her head. He was convicted of manslaughter, but skipped town and was given a suspended sentence.

NEGLECT, DECAY AND DISINTEGRATION

A walk anywhere in town will make one thing obvious: the earth is none too stable here. Lurching slabs of concrete, meandering cracks, and unexpected gaps in the pavement are everywhere, even along elegant Paseo de la Reforma. Roots of sturdy rubber trees burst through concrete and massive colonial churches tilt and sag into the soft ground. The city has a feel of a drawing done with an unsteady hand. Built on a lake in Aztec times, the land was bundled together into many small islands, like Venice. (You can still see this original landscape in Xochimilco.) Since the Aztecs did not use pack animals or the wheel, boats became a primary means of transport. Long since paved over, the soft liquid substructure of the city is still evident on its surface, rattled by occasional seismic activity. Scars from the deadly earthquake of 1985 are still found in parts of the city.

Buildings with tilted walls, crumbling facades, rusting metalwork, broken planters, cracked and bulging sidewalks are common sights in Mexico City, the effect often heightened by a proximity to some gleaming new high-rise. There is a notable tendency here to let things go to rack and ruin, financial investment be damned. Depending on the mood I'm in, I can see it as a charming reminder of the temporal nature of all cities, or an indication of a complete lack of civic pride. But there is no denying that decrepitude is one of the characteristics that defines Mexico City.

Among the the most remarkable examples of this is the high-rise Edificio Insurgentes (Insurgentes 300, between Zacatecas and Guanajuato), known by many here as the Canada Building, for a huge sign that used to crown its top. Inaugurated in 1958, it was the most fashionable address in its day for the offices of politicians, doctors and lawyers.

Its heyday lasted about 10 years, and then things started to go downhill. The earthquake of 1985 was the nail in the coffin, but a fire, and a murder of a tenant didn't help.

Insurgentes 300, also known by its official original name, Condominio Insurgentes, Col. Roma.

Spirits of those killed in the fire supposedly haunt the 15th and 16th floors.

Elevators no longer work, graffiti covers much of the ground floor, and upper floors are a hodge-podge of slapdash additions and makeshift alterations. In 2012 the city ejected the remaining tenants and closed the building. Rumor has it that it was being used as a halfway house for illegal immigrants from Nicaragua. Take a look from across the street to fully appreciate the weirdness of this once grand edifice.

But all this physical instability has created a flexible and resilient culture. Mexicans are the most Buddhist-like of westerners, embracing instability, change, and death as normal parts of daily life, and as a result they seem remarkably calm. The phrase '*ni modo*' (literally "no way," sort of a resigned shrug) is more often heard in response to situations beyond one's control than anything more aggressive or confrontational. A popular song by the beloved ranchera composer José Alfredo Jimenez has the refrain "*no vale nada la vida*" (life is worth nothing), sung to a sweet and lilting waltz melody. Mexicans of all ages know it well.

POLANCO

Polanco, which extends along the north side of Chapultepec Park, is home to some of the wealthiest people in Mexico. It houses some of the best hotels, restaurants, and shops in the city and is the location of choice for many foreign embassies, international corporations as well as a large portion of the city's Jewish community.

Near to many of the top museums, the air of sophisticated culture extends even to its streets, named after philosophers, writers, and scientists. Avenida Presidente Masaryk, named after a former Czech leader, is often compared to New York's Fifth Avenue or Los Angeles' Rodeo Drive, with its lineup of status conscious stores like Tiffany's, Gucci, Cartier, and Louis Vuitton.

Development of the area began back in the 1930's, but the big building boom escalated in the 1950's, and continues today. Designed as a purely residential area at first, homes in Polanco were marketed to those wishing to emulate an American lifestyle—freestanding houses had front and back yards, a novelty back then. Examples of the original architecture, a florid style with ornately sculpted doorways and windows known as Colonial Californiano, are scattered throughout the neighborhood, although many have been turned into stores and offices.

Boutiques Masaryk, Polanco.

Polanco suffers a bit from a reputation as a snooty place—there's even a popular restaurant named 'Snob'. A few years back, the 'Ladies of Polanco' became famous after a video on YouTube went viral showing two wealthy residents berating a dark-skinned transit policeman for daring to give them a ticket. It was the talk of the town for several weeks. But there's no denying that Polanco is a defining element of Mexico City, and well worth a visit to see how 'the other half' (or at least the top 3%) lives.

WALKING TOUR #14:
Polanco

Two metro stops (Polanco and Auditorio) serve Polanco on the #7 line, but neither is very convenient for a walking tour. Arriving by taxi, ask your driver to take you via **Campos Eliseos**, a lovely tree-lined street lined with several high end hotels that gives you a quick overview of the luxurious life-styles enjoyed by many here. Ask the driver to leave you at the corner of Julio Verne and **Parque Lincoln**, just next to a taxi sitio you can use later on this tour.

Parque Linclon

Polanquito, the area around Parque Lincoln, is the closest thing to a town center, and the best place to walk around and get a feel for the neighborhood. In the park you'll find an art gallery, an aviary, and a small pool where kids play with toy sailboats. The nearby streets, Virgilio, Julio Verne, Oscar Wilde and Alexandre Dumas are lined with upmarket stores and restaurants, and lots of well-heeled customers. At Masaryk 360, walk into the **Pasaje Polanco**, a former apartment complex turned into a shopping mall, which feels like a bit of old Palm

Francisco J. Serrano's Pasaje Polanco along Avenida Presidente Masaryk.

Beach in Mexico City (Snob is here). It was designed in 1939 by Francisco Serrano, the architect of many of the best art deco buildings in Colonia Condesa.

Emilio Castelar runs along the north side of Parque Lincoln. There are some great examples of extravagant Colonial Californiano architecture here. It's worth poking inside to get a glimpse of the splendor of these former residences, even though they've been remodeled as stores and restaurants—the glamour of yesteryear is still evident amidst the layers of contemporary posh. As you walk west on Emilio Castelar (toward Edgar Allan Poe), you'll find these old houses at #135, #149, and #163.

Besides Polanquito, the other area well worth visiting is the ultra-modern development of stores, offices, and museums in the northwest corner of Polanco known as **Plaza Carso**. Here you'll see a futurist version of Mexico that stands in extreme contrast to its image of old-style colonial charm.

It's a long hike from Polanquito, so take a taxi from the sitio in the middle of Parque Lincoln (on Julio Verne, in front of the statue of Martin Luther King, Jr.). Go to the main entrance of the **Centro Commercial Antara** (Ejército Nacional near Moliere), the snazziest shopping mall in town. During one visit I heard the voice of Ella Fitzgerald singing 'My Heart Stood Still.' Mine almost did, too, when I saw some of the price tags. There's a pleasant open-air food court—better for people watching than dining. The Cinemex movie theater upstairs features reclining leather seats and waiter service—you can order from a 10-page menu.

Leave the mall by the passageway to the left of where you entered, across from the Hugo Boss store. Outside, across the street, you'll see **Plaza Carso**, a recent development of shops, offices, and apartments. The big draw here is the **Jumex Collection,** Mexico City's most important contemporary art museum. It features big-name artists in exhibitions that change every month or so. Check their website for information (www.fundacionjumex.org). There are great views from the second floor terrace.

Next door to the Jumex Collection is the **Museo Soumaya**, pet project of Mexican billionaire Carlos Slim (his son-in-law designed the sinuous, metal-clad structure). The collection is a grab bag, near-masterworks to kitsch, but there are some notable European paintings (by El Greco, Reubens, Tintoretto, and Zurburán for example), a number of Rodins, and a delightful selection of pre-Hispanic ceramic vases and sculptures. The best way to see this museum is to take the elevator from the lobby to the top floor and work your way down.

Museo Soumaya

ALSO WORTH A LOOK IN POLANCO

Librería El Péndulo
(Alejandro Dumas 81) is a bookstore/cafe with a small, but savvy selection in English books.

David Alfaro Siquerios Museum
(Tres Picos 29). A contemporary art museum with changing exhibits.

W Hotel
(Campos Eliseos 252). The bar here is one of the top 'beautiful people' spots in the city.

MAP store
(Emilio Castelar at Temístocles). The store of the Museo de Arte Popular in the Centro carries good quality Mexican handicrafts.

Panadería Da Silva
(Oscar Wilde 12). The bread and pastries at this Portuguese style bakery are excellent.

Art Galleries
see: 'The Art Scene' p. 108

ZONA ROSA

This area is often thought of as an important tourist destination, but I don't find myself drawn to its atmosphere of globalized commerce. It's a popular lunch destination for local businessmen and politicians. From the 1940's through the 1960's it was the glamorous residential and nightlife area of the city, but it has gotten a bit tacky over the years. Many international restaurants, hotels, and stores will make you feel like you are still at home. It is, however, the center of gay social life—check out Calle Amberes (near Reforma) with its cafés, restaurants, bars, and shops. It's also the center for Korean immigrants, who have opened many restaurants and several food shops in the area, especially along the western stretch of Calle Hamburgo. The best place to eat in the area is the venerable Fonda el Refugio, at Liverpool 166.

There's a weekend flea market at the Plaza del Angel (between Hamburgo and Londres near Amberes) with some high-end antiques.

The nearest metro stop is Insurgentes on the #1 line.

Gay Pride March

HEADING SOUTH:
Coyoacán, San Ángel, Tlalpan and Xochimilco

These four areas all lie to the south of Mexico City. Any two of them could be comfortably seen in one day.

COYOACÁN

About 10km south of the Zócalo is the village of Coyoacán ("Place of the Coyotes" in Nahuatl), which, although long since swallowed up into the greater metropolis, still preserves an aura of small town colonial charm. Near the university, it is a favored place for professors to live, adding to its reputation of bohemian sophistication. Frida Kahlo's big blue house is here, as well as one of the best traditional markets in the city. Visiting Coyoacán during the week is a peaceful event; weekends have a fun, bustling atmosphere, but go early to avoid crowds.

WALKING TOUR #15:
Frida's Neighborhood

To go by metro, take the #3 train to the Viveros/Derechos Humans stop—don't be tempted to get out at the more logical Coyoacán stop. Use the exit marked Viveros de Coyoacán. You will be on Avenida Universidad, walking against the direction of the traffic. Go one long block, cross G. Pérez Valenzuela (which appears as Progreso on some maps) until you reach a small stone bridge (no street sign, but there's a big OXXO store across the street).

Cross over the bridge, head right and walk down Calle Parras, which is lined with high-walled homes and secret gardens. Turn right when you reach Calle Salvador Novo, then left on **Francisco Sosa**, one of the principal streets in Coyoacán. (If you arrive by taxi, start the tour here). At this corner is Casa Alvarado, an 18th century residence decorated with *ajaracas*, bas-relief patterns that are a characteristic of local colonial architecture.

It is now the **Fonoteca Nacional,** a 'museum of sound'. Exhibits change but you can check their website for events and concerts (*www.fonotecanacional.gob.mx*). A mini-plaza across the street offers a better view of this impressive building.

As you walk along Francisco Sosa, you'll pass an art gallery, a chocolate shop, a children's clothing store—just the sort of things you'd expect in this quaint village-like place. As you pass #238, notice the enormous trees, which reveal the age of this ancient neighborhood.

A bit further ahead is **Plaza Santa Caterina**, one of the most charming spots in the city, best experienced from a park bench. There is a small church and a couple of nice places to eat.

Across the street from the church, walk into the lovely garden of the **Casa de la Cultura Jesús Reyes Heroles**, a cultural center in a former private home. (If you want to conserve on walking, you might hail a taxi here and ride to the central plaza of Coyoacán—about 6 blocks straight ahead along Francisco Sosa.)

Santa Catarina Church

The Instituto Italiano de Cultura (#77) and Los Talleres (#29), a dance school, both have charming back garden cafes. The DIF building (#19) has some interesting brickwork.

At the end of Francisco Sosa, you'll see yellow arches straight ahead of you as you reach the main plaza of Coyoacán, which is divided in two halves, **El Jardín Centenario** and **Jardín Hidalgo**.

Straight ahead is the **church of San Juan Bautista**, a highly gilded baroque affair, with a peaceful cloister. This part of the plaza has vendors selling balloons, toys, and traditional sweets and it's pleasant to stroll around or just sit and watch the world go by as you listen to the organ grinders.

Across the plaza to the left of the church is the so-called **Casa de Cortés**, which occupies the site of Cortes' home, but the actual building dates from 1755. Today, this big yellow edifice houses municipal offices, including a tourist bureau just as you enter, where you can get a good map of the area.

At the far end of the plaza (behind the church) you will see **La Guadalupana**, a cantina in business since 1932, once a favorite hangout of Frida Kahlo and Diego Rivera. Just beyond the restaurant on the right (Calle Higuera) is the **Mercado de Antojitos**, where you find many traditional Mexican foods. There are several stands with good pozole, and at #14 the best deep-fried quesadillas I've eaten—try *flor de calabaza* (squash blossom flowers) or *huitlacoche* (corn fungus.)

Walk down Avenida Hidalgo (to the left of La Guadalupana). Half a block down is the **Museo de Culturas Populares** (closed Mondays), which has excellent temporary exhibits on various aspects of Mexican culture as well as a good bookstore. (*www.museoculturaspopulares.gob.mx*)

Head back to the main plaza, turn right on Allende and walk 3 blocks to the main market. Along the way you will pass the Restaurante El Morral, a good choice for traditional Mexican dishes (excellent hand-made tortillas) and locally famous Café El Jarocho where they have been roasting coffee beans since 1953.

The **Coyoacán Market** is one of the most picturesque in the city and it has some of the best market food—there are stalls inside the market as well as outside along Malintzín. Enter by Pasillo 9 and walk straight ahead to the middle of the market to find the justly renowned **Tostadas Coyoacán** (don't get confused by the nearby competitors which are

Arcos del Jardin del Centennario

Frida Kahlo Museum

not as good). Crisp tortillas are piled up with a variety of ingredients, which you will see laid out on the counter. A big selection of fresh-fruit *aguas frescas* is available, too.

In one corner of the market you will find baskets, pottery, and birdcages for sale. Another corner features a popular outdoor seafood restaurant, **El Jardín del Pulpo**, with long communal tables.

Leaving the market, continue along Allende two blocks to Londres, where you will see the **Museo Frida Kahlo** (*www.museofridakahlo.org.mx*) with its famous blue walls. There's a better collection of her work in the Museo Dolores Olmedo in Xochimilco, but the house and garden are interesting, and for Frida fans it's a must-see.

There is a taxi sitio just outside the museum on Allende, or if you walk back to the main plaza, there's one behind the big church. If you're heading on to the sights below or further south to Xochimilco, you might consider hiring a driver by the hour—it costs around US$10 per hour.

OFF THE BEATEN TRACK IN COYOACÁN

The Cineteca Nacional at the northern edge of Coyoacán *(Avenida México-Coyoacán 389, near Rio Churobusco—take a taxi or walk from Metro Coyoacán)* shows an interesting mix of international films, new and old, in an eight-theater complex with bookstore and café. Look for listings in Tiempo Libre magazine, or visit *www.cinetecanacional.net*

Plaza de la Conchita A few blocks from the main plaza (walk down Higuera) is the lovely, peaceful park and church of la Conchita, one of the oldest in the city. This crumbling gem is a rare example of *tequitqui*, which shows the influence of indigenous Indian craftsmen on Spanish baroque architectural ornament.

Museo León Trotsky *(Rio Churubusco 410 near Gómez Farías)* The famous Russian revolutionary leader lived in Mexico from 1937 until his assassination in 1940. His house was left untouched since then—you can still see the bullet holes. It's about five blocks from Frida's house.

Museo Diego Rivera Anahuacalli *(Calle Museo 150, Colonia San Pablo Tepetlapa, tel. 5617-4310, www.museoanahuacalli.org.mx)* Rivera built this studio and museum space, a few miles south of Coyoacán, incorporating distinctive elements of pre-Hispanic architecture. The building is fascinating, as is his fine collection of pre-Hispanic art. If you are visiting around Dia de Muertos, you will see one of the city's most elaborate altars. From Coyoacán, the museum is best reached by car or taxi, but you can take a bus down Avenida División del Norte, getting off at Calle de Museo—it's a bit of a hike from there.

Anahuacalli Museum

TIME AND SPACE

Mexicans enjoy being in groups, and move easily through crowds, rarely pushing, shoving, or yelling at each other. Public behavior is usually contained, but great value is placed on heartfelt emotion. Grief and joy are expressed with exuberance that would be considered crass in some societies —wailing cries are heard in mariachi songs and actors in *telenovelas* (Mexican soap operas) burst into tears every few minutes. Fiestas, both public and private, are a regular part of life. Even death is celebrated with much ado—

Día de Muertos being one of the most important holidays of the year. Anger, however, is not considered appropriate for public display, and "saving face" is very important. Mexicans do not like to say no, which can cause much confusion with foreign visitors. For example, it is considered more polite to accept an invitation to a party and not show up than to refuse the invitation.

The relationship to time is another element that distinguishes Mexican life. The saying "Time is money" makes no sense here—they are two very distinct concepts. Being late for most social engagements is not considered rude, and speed is not highly valued (except in one's car.) One of the few instances where the foreign visitor will notice speed is at the end of a meal in a restaurant. Waiters often whisk away plates while the last bite of food is heading toward your mouth, so watch out (although you are always invited to remain at the table for as long as you like, and a check is rarely presented without being requested).

SAN ANGEL

Like its neighbor Coyoacán, San Angel retains its small town feeling with cobblestone streets and an attractive colonial-period plaza, although the commercial crush of the city impinges a bit more here. A weekday visit allows you to experience its small-town qualities. On weekends the main plaza fills with street vendors and tourists, the atmosphere is more lively and carnival like. You can easily visit both San Angel and Coyoacán in one day.

View at the Plaza del Carmen.

WALKING TOUR #16:
San Angel

If arriving from Coyoacán, take a taxi or a bus heading west on Miguel Angel de Quevedo. If you're coming from the Centro, take a taxi or the metrobus down Insurgentes to Avenida de la Paz (Bombilla stop on the metrobus), where this walking tour begins.

☛ **Walk along Avenida de la Paz** (you'll see Sanborn's at the corner) toward the center of San Angel. The best restaurants are on this street—Paxia and El Cardenal are both good choices.

Ex-convent of El Carmen.

When you reach busy Avenida Revolución, go left, past the church, and visit the **Museo del Carmen**, a 17th century convent, one of the treasures of colonial architecture in Mexico City. The massive building has a calm, somewhat austere, atmosphere, and a lovely garden in back. There's a good collection of religious art. Don't miss the mummies in the cellar.

After visiting the museum, bravely cross Avenida Revolución, and walk along the left side of the small park until you reach the **Plaza San Jacinto**, the main plaza of San Angel (there's a taxi sitio right at the corner). Walk straight ahead, along the left side of the park.

(When you reach the end of the plaza, you can zig-zag left, then right where you'll see the main commercial strip of San Angel, where the 'real people' shop in this generally upscale area. The red colonnaded building at the end of the street is the market, with a few good taco stands under the arches.)

Saturday art market in Plaza San Jacinto.

Walk around the plaza clockwise until you reach #18 bis, the back entry to the **Parróquia de San Jacinto**, and wander through the red and white cloister, lovely gardens, and the gilded baroque chapel. The place emits the energy from centuries of prayer.

Exit through the church garden, turning left on Juarez and left again on Arboles. A third left turn will bring you to the 2a Cerrada de Frontera, which leads to the intimate **Plaza de Los Arcángeles,** a tranquil residential enclave, completely removed from the choas of the city. It's especially beautiful in March/April when the jacarandas are in bloom. You can backtrack to the church, or take the Cerrada on the other side of the park (far right from where you entered) which will lead you to Frontera—go left here to return to Plaza San Jacinto.

The plaza itself is 'almost pretty', but the abundance of iron fences gives it a caged-in feel. On the east side of the plaza, next to the taxi stand, take a look at the **Museo Casa del Risco**, a cultural center which has temporary art exhibits and a good collection of colonial art and furniture upstairs. The main draw here is the fanciful fountain in the patio, a fantasy collage of ceramic plates and seashells. Entry is free.

Baroque fountain in Casa del Risco.

After exploring the plaza, take a taxi to the **San Angel Inn**, a former hacienda, now a restaurant. The short ride takes you along the cobblestone streets past large, elegant homes. The old world atmosphere at the Inn is great, the food is acceptable, and the margaritas are said to be the best in the city.

At Plaza de San Jacinto.

Across the street is the **Museo Casa-Estudio Diego Rivera y Frida Kahlo**, Rivera's last home, designed by Juan O'Gorman in 1931. There's not a lot of art by either artist here, but it gives you a peek into their lives. The modernist architecture does not suggest a cozy home life, but as geometric sculpture, it's fascinating. (O'Gorman is famous for his huge ceramic murals at the University a few miles south, and his panoramic historical murals at the Castillo in Chapultepec Park.)

Avenida Altavista, the wide asphalt road in front of the Casa-Estudio, is the high end shopping street of San Angel.

The doorman at the restaurant or museum can call you a taxi when you are ready to leave.

OTHER ATTRACTIONS IN SAN ANGEL

Bazar Sábado This handicraft market takes place on Saturdays only in a labyrinthine building just to the left of the Museo Casa del Risco on the main plaza. You're unlikely to leave this place empty handed, but go before noon to avoid the crowds.

Museo de Arte Carrillo Gil (Av. Revolución 1608 at Altavista, www.museodeartecarrillogil.com, closed Mondays) has changing exhibits of contempory art, as well as a small but impressive collection of 20th century Mexican masters.

Plaza Loreto this interesting shopping mall built in an old paper factory, is a short ride from the main plaza. There's a branch of the Museo Soumaya there and the Taberna de León, one of the best restaurants in San Angel, located in the home of the paper mill's former owner.

XOCHIMILCO

At the southern edge of Mexico City (about 20km from the Centro) is the village of Xochimilco, now absorbed into the metropolitan area. You can happily spend a full day here visiting three main attractions: the Museo Dolores Olmedo Patiño, the market, and the so-called Floating Gardens. The gardens refer to *chinampas*, which date back to pre-Hispanic times. These are small islands created by enclosing an area of the lake with a basketry fence, then rooting plants within the perimeter and mounding compost on top to create highly fertile planting grounds. Plant and flower growers live and work here, as they have for centuries. Colorful wooden pole-boats called *trajineras* can be rented to glide through the network of canals created by the chinampas. On weekends there is a festive atmosphere as hundreds of families take to the canals, along with floating mariachis, food and drink vendors, and souvenir sellers. During the week it is much quieter, although still lively. Sundays are most crowded. The classic 1944 Mexican movie *Maria Candelaria*, starring Dolores Del Río as an Indian flower seller, is filled with wonderfully romantic images of the Xochimilco of yesteryear.

Colorful trajineras (rafts) on Lake Xochimilco.

Museo Dolores Olmedo Patiño *(Avenida Mexico 5843, La Noria, Xochimilco, tel. 5555-0891).* This is one of my favorite museums anywhere, great art in a beautiful setting. Dolores Olmedo, a rich socialite patron of Diego Rivera, opened her house and collection to the public in 1994. Wandering through the beautifully landscaped grounds with strutting peacocks and waddling ducks, you arrive at the 16th century hacienda. Out front is a fenced-off area where several *xoloitzcuintzles*, rare hairless dogs of pre-Hispanic origin, are frolicking or sleeping. The ceramic sculptures of these dogs from the state of Colima are a highlight

of the museum's small but impressive pre-Hispanic collection. You'll find a good sampling of works by Diego Rivera here, including a roomful of luscious small paintings of sunsets and some excellent lithographs. Frida Kahlo has her own room, the single largest collection of her work—far better than what you will find in Frida's own house in Coyoacán (although works are often loaned out to other museums). At the end is an exhibit of Mexican handicrafts, also of high quality, and a pleasant outdoor snack bar. The peacocks wander freely here—more than once I have been within a few feet of a full-feather display.

Olmedo lived on the property until her death in 2002. Her less interesting private quarters are now open to the public: too many Chinese antiques and too many photos of herself looking rather imperious.

See *www.museodoloresolmedo.org.mx* for more information and a map to get there—make a copy for your taxi driver if going by cab as almost everyone has trouble finding this place.

Getting there: *Many hotels offer tours of Xochimilco by taxi or mini-van, or you can engage a taxi by the hour at any sitio. You can also reach the museum by metro. Take the #2 line to the last stop, Tasqueña, then switch to the tren ligero, an above-ground extension of the metro. Get off at La Noria station and ask directions there—it's a short walk.*

Getting to the center of Xochimilco: You can hail a cab in front of the museum or take any of the small green buses marked Xochimilco which go along Avenida Guadalupe Ramírez. You will know when to get off when you see the white dome of the church ahead of you. Flanking the entrance to the church are the two halves of the town plaza. On the left is **Jardín Juárez** with its gazebo, gardens, and benches. On the right is **Jardín Morelos**, which has been given over to vendors, many selling pirated CD's and DVD's. The weekend cacophony here is most impressive. The bustling **Mercado de Xochimilco** is just behind the row of tall palm trees. It's one of the best markets in the city.

The **market** consists of two buildings, both marked with tall *Mi Mercado* signs. The one facing the plaza is marked *Xochitl Zona* and contains mostly fruits, vegetables, and meats, with a few good pottery

stalls outside. The other building, *Xochimilco Anexo*, is just behind the first. Here you will find plants, flowers, and several small fondas serving inexpensive Mexican food. Both are classic examples of neighborhood Mexican markets, lively, and colorful. Between the two market buildings on the right (Calle Morales) is the lovely **El Rosario** church, a little gem perfect for a moment of tranquility.

Tlacoyos in Mercado de Xochimilco.

Floating Gardens

From the market you can walk or take a pedicab to several nearby *embarcaderos* (boat landings) where you can rent a boat for a canal ride. Young men may solicit you to accompany them to a specific embarcadero and will help you arrange a boat rental—they may seem suspect, but don't worry, they are just doing their job. They are paid a small commission by the boat owner. Prices for boats are posted and will vary depending on the size of the boat and the length of the tour (one hour minimum)—be sure to agree on the total price before you set out. A small tip for the boatman is customary.

Woman in a chalupa selling plants.

Mariachis playing for tourists on the canals

If you need a taxi, there is a sitio on Calle Miguel Hidalgo near Pino, not far from the Jardín Juarez. It is slightly obscured by street vendors— look for it near the entrance of the Bodega Commercial Mexicana.

Cows grazing along a canal

TLALPAN

Like its neighbors to the north, Coyoacán and San Ángel, Tlalpan is an old pueblo that still retains some colonial charm even as the city has grown around it. It is worth a visit for its pretty main plaza, the bustling market, and a cultural center with art exhibits (sometimes).

But the top attraction in Tlalpan is the **Capilla de las Capuchinas** designed by renowned Mexican architect Luis Barragán in the 1950's. On visiting the chapel my eyes welled up with tears—something that has happened to me while experiencing other art forms, but never architecture. The space Barragán created has a sublime beauty that suggests a divine presence.

The architect's trademarks are all here: contrast of low, shadowy spaces with high, bright ones; the use of reflected light to create Rothko-like colors (the chapel glows with a light that simultaneously suggests both sunrise and sunset); a sensitive mix of natural materials. "Even the temperature of a room was important to him," the young nun who guided us said, as we stood in the small, dark, chilly anteroom of the chapel. Barragán has created an intimate theater for prayer. His clear visual poetry is filled with optimism for a world beyond our own that might really exist.

You must call and make an appointment to visit the chapel. It's open weekdays only; telephone 5573-2395, "donation" 60 pesos.

The chapel is located at Miguel Hidalgo 43, just a few blocks from the main plaza of Tlalpan. There's a Metrobús stop (Insurgentes Line #1, 'Fuentes Brotantes') within walking distance.

HEADING NORTH:
Tlatelolco, the Basílica, and Teotihuacán

These three places are best visited as a single day trip with a car and driver.

TLATELOLCO

A short distance north of the Centro Histórico are the pre-Hispanic ruins of the former Mexica city-state of Tlatelolco, dating back to the 14th century. It is part of the **Plaza de las Tres Culturas**. The Spanish colonial church of Santiago (17th century), and contemporary Mexican buildings are the other two elements in this cultural triad. This is also where, on October 2, 1968, government forces killed more than 300

Plaza de las Tres Culturas

unarmed student protesters. The area has an eerie calm about it that reflects this history.

The main modern buildings here house the **Centro Cultural Universitario Tlatelolco**, which houses several museums. There is a memorial to the 1968 massacre and a museum of the archeological site on the ground floor—both rather didactic (Spanish only).

The best reason to visit Tlatelolco is hidden upstairs in the tower building. The excellent **Coleccíon Stavenhagen** displays more than 500 pieces of pre-Hispanic art from all over Mexico, some of them surprisingly comical.

Museum hours: Tuesday to Sunday, 10 to 6 (the church is closed from 1 to 4 during the week). Entry cost: 30 pesos, free on Sundays, www.tlatelolco.unam.mx

BASÍLICA DE LA VIRGIN DE GUADALUPE

Around ninety percent of Mexicans are Catholic. There is no more powerful image for Mexican Catholics than La Virgen de Guadalupe. She is so beloved that both girls and boys are named after her, and millions of pilgrims visit her each year, some crawling the last miles on hands and knees. Her titles include 'Queen of Mexico', 'Patroness of the Americas', and 'Empress of Latin America', among others. Her image is everywhere in Mexico. Tough-looking tattooed macho guys will cross themselves as they pass her image, taxi drivers have her as a constant passenger, dangling from the mirror, and her altar protects every neighborhood market. It is almost impossible to overestimate her influence.

A visit to her Basílica is a must to understand Mexico. The church, built in the 1970's, is the work of Pedro Ramírez Vázquez, who also designed the Anthropology museum. It looks a bit like a Las Vegas nightclub, and the miraculous shroud—an image of the Virgin that appeared on the cloak of the peasant Juan Diego in 1531— is viewed from a conveyor belt, adding an element of shopping mall or airport to the religious trappings. You may see Aztec-clad concheros dancing and singing out front—all part of the confusing hybrid of Mexican Catholicism.

But nearby the awkwardly tilting **Colegiata** and the tile-crowned **El Pocito** church are beautiful colonial era buildings worth noting. More than the sights, however, it is the ambience, equally fervent and festive, that makes this place worth visiting.

The nearest metro is La Villa-Basílica station on the #6 line. You can also take the Metrobús (line #1) north on Insurgentes to Deportivo 18 de Marzo, then walk about five blocks west. You'll see the top of the Basílica from the pedestrian bridge as you exit.

December 12 is the feast day of the Virgin of Guadalupe, when upwards of a million devotees visit the place.

TEOTIHUACÁN

About 35 miles northeast of the city are the remains of the ancient civilization of Teotihuacán, one of the most impressive sites of a vanished culture anywhere in the world. The city flourished from about 100 to 750 A.D. with population estimates as high as 200,000. By the time the Aztecs arrived in the area, it had been abandoned for 700 years, although they cleverly appropriated its history as their own, claiming it as the birth and burial place of their gods. The broad, serene spaces and the simple grandeur of the architecture give the site an awe-inspiring power. The so-called **Pyramid of the Sun** is the 3rd largest pyramid in the world, after Cholula in Mexico and Cheops in Egypt. There are some interesting carved details and fragments of painted murals in situ, and two separate museums, one of artifacts,

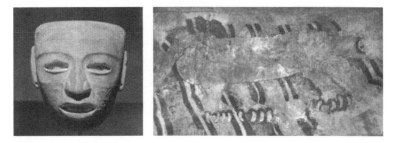

one of mural painting (I find the exhibits in the Museo de Antropología even better, however.) The **Palacio de Quetzalpapálotl** has the most interesting interior spaces. Maps, guide books, and all kinds of tacky souvenirs are available as you enter the ruins.

Plan at least 6 hours for a visit, including transportation time. Sitio and hotel taxis will take you for prices starting around US$45 per person, but you can also go by bus from Terminal Norte for about US$8 per person, round trip. Autobuses Teotihuacán leave every 15 to 30 minutes (starting at 7am) from the far end of the bus station, near Sala 8. The last bus leaves the ruins at 6pm. Bring a hat, water, and sunscreen as there is no shade at all at the ruins and you will walk several miles to cover the entire area. There are many restaurants on the road circling the ruins—an interesting choice is **La Gruta**, located in a cool cave by Puerta 5. On January 1 and the spring and summer solstices, thousands flock to the ruins, so be aware that traffic may be horrendous on those days.

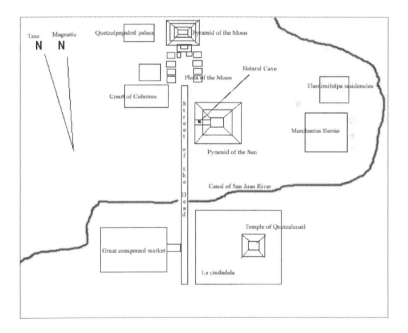

OTHER INTERESTING PLACES TO VISIT

Casa/Estudio Luís Barragán

Luis Barragán

(General Francisco Ramírez 14, Colonia Tacubaya. Call for appointment, 5515-4908, www.casaluisbarragan.org). Mexico's important and influential architect Luis Barragán (1902-1988) combined elements of modernism with traditional Mexican materials. A visit to his home and studio, which was named a UNESCO World Heritage Site in 2004, is a sublime and mystical architectural experience. *Taxis might have a hard time " finding this place, so bring a map, or take the metro #7 to Constituyentes and follow the sidewalk alongside the traffic on Avenida Constituyentes one block to Francisco Ramírez.*

Plaza de Danzón *(Plaza de la Ciudadela, metro Balderas on the #1 or #3 lines.)* There is dancing in the street every Saturday afternoon (starting at noon). You will see hundreds of people of all ages engaged in danzón, a restrained and demanding form of ballroom dance with roots in the Caribbean state of Veracruz. You can join in the fun with free group classes. I highly recommend this weekly event, which is oddly touching and heart-warming.

Casa de la Bola *(Parque Lira 136, Colonia Tacubaya, near metro Tacubaya on the #1 or #7 line)* This colonial mansion redone in sumptuous 19th-century style is one of the hidden gems of the city, a good place to dream of times past and for a moment of tranquility strolling through adjacent Parque Lira. *It is open only on Sunday from 11 to 5, or by appointment (call 5515-5582).*

Centro Nacional de las Artes (CENART)

Secretaría de Comunicaciones y Transportes *(Avenida Xola near Eje Central, the nearest metro is Etiopia on the #3 line, then take a local bus).* This architectural complex of government office buildings, which dates from 1953, was severely damaged in the 1985 earthquake, but has since been repaired. The mosaic stone murals depicting episodes from Mexican history, of epic proportions, are justly famous. Be sure to check out the heroic figurative sculptures adorning the entryway.

Centro Nacional de las Artes (CENART). *(Rio Churubusco at Tlalpan, metro Ermita on the #2 line).* Anyone interested in modern architecture will love taking a stroll through this campus, where you can see buildings by several of Mexico's prominent late 20th-century architects. It is the most important art school in the country, with faculties in painting, sculpture, cinema, music, and dance. Look for frequent concert and dance events listed in *Tiempo Libre* magazine.

Mucho Mundo Chocolate
(Milan 45, Colonia Juárez, www.mucho. org.mx). There's a lot of history and didactic material, but the best thing here is a little room completely lined in chocolate.

DAY OF THE DEAD IN MEXICO CITY

Benjamin Franklin had never been to Mexico when he wrote, "In this world nothing is certain except death and taxes". With big business tax loopholes, and an estimated 59% of the workforce in the non-taxpaying 'informal economy', the only certainty here is death. Each year on Día de Muertos, Mexicans face that inevitability head-on.

My first experience of Día de Muertos was years ago in San Miguel de Allende. I waited patiently in a long line of flower-laden visitors to pass through the narrow gateway. Visits to gravesites in the U.S. were dark, sad, and solemn events, with no encouragement to linger. In Mexico, upon entering the vast field of tombstones, it seemed more like a big party, a bit subdued, but festive, colorful, bustling. There were flowers everywhere, candles flickering, guitar players strumming, people eating, talking, praying, laughing, and only a few of them crying.

With its roots deep in the pre-Christian past, Mexico's attitude toward death presents one of the strongest contrasts to that of its northern neighbors. Nobel laureate Octavio Paz wrote, "The word death is not pronounced in New York, in Paris, in London, because it burns the lips. The Mexican, in contrast, is familiar with death, jokes about it, caresses it, sleeps with it, celebrates it; it is one of his favorite toys and his most steadfast love."

La Catarina, is one of the most popular figures of the Day of the Dead celebrations in Mexico.

Famed 19th century artist José Guadalupe Posada created a popular image of death, La Calaca Catrina, that shows up everywhere. With her big feathered hat and wide grin, she looks more like Carol Channing in Hello Dolly than any frightening image of the Grim Reaper. The curious phrase *Feliz Día de los Muertos* shows up on sugar skulls and greeting cards. Death in Mexico, while not exactly a friend, is certainly a member of the family.

Indigenous peoples believed that the soul did not die, but moved on to a resting place known as *Mictlán*, from whence it could be summoned home to visit friends and relatives. Before the Spanish conquest, the return of departed souls was celebrated in July and August. The Spaniards changed the date to coincide with All Souls' Day of the Catholic Church, leaving the newly baptized natives with only two days, November 1 and 2, during which they welcome home the deceased. The first day is devoted to departed children, the next to adults.

It's a long way from Mictlán, so the living must appeal to all the senses of the dearly departed to help them find their way home. Food, flowers, incense, music, even cigarettes and alcohol are used to create altars, known as *ofrendas* in homes and public spaces all over Mexico. You don't have to be Mexican to participate in Day of the Dead rituals, however. Visiting a cemetery or preparing an altar at home can be done by anyone.

Day of the Dead alter.

Woman lighting copal incense at the cemetery.

Flowers, including Mexican marigolds, used in the celebration of the Day of the Dead.

One of the best places to stock up on all the necessary items for a home altar is the Mercado Jamaica (*Avenida Morelos and Congreso de la Unión, metro stop Jamaica on the #9 line*). As the city's wholesale flower market, the quantity of marigolds, coxcombs and other flowers is staggering. Booths set up around the perimeter of the market offer sugar figurines, candles, incense, food, papel picado (die-cut tissue paper), and other items used to create altars.

Altars are set up between October 28 and 30, and dismantled promptly on November 3, when Death is given a holiday until next year.

Although celebrations in rural areas of Oaxaca and Michoacán are often written about, Day of the Dead in Mexico City occurs on a scale befitting one of the planet's biggest cities. Getting into the main cemeteries in Mexico City can be a daunting proposition, but altars are set up all over town. You'll see them in markets, shopping malls, metro stops, banks, hotels, school, hospitals, and outside every Delegación office.

Here are some special places known for their elaborate altars:

The Zócalo, the city's main plaza in the Centro Histórico

Museo Anahuacalli, Coyoacán *(www.museoanahuacalli.org.mx)*

Claustro of Sor Juana *(Izazaga 92, near Isabel la Católica in the Centro)*

Museo de las Culturas *(Calle Mondea, Centro)*

Plaza Juárez *(on the south side of the Alameda)*

Museo de la Ciudad *(Pino Suárez 30, Centro)*

Plaza Cívica del Museo Panteón de San Fernando
(Plaza de San Fernando 17, Colonia Guerrero, near Metro Hidalgo)

UNAM *(on the esplanade near the Rectoría)*

Part of the "megaofrenda" at UNAM.

WHAT TO DO AT NIGHT

Lively clusters of bars and restaurants are to be found along Av. Álvaro Obregón in Colonia Roma and Av. Michoacán in Colonia Condesa. The scene in the Centro is more spread out—look under Bars and Cantinas for places there.

Check listings in Tiempo Libre or Chilango magazines for current art, dance, theater and music events. *www.ticketmaster.com.mx* is a source for ticketed events. In the space marked BUSCAR search the following places for current and upcoming performances: Palacio de Bellas Artes, Teatro de la Ciudad, El Lunario, Teatro Metropolitán.

Noche de Museos On the last Wednesday of each month, many museums stay open until 10 p.m. Check the website for more information: www.cultura.df.gob.mx/nochedemuseos

Palacio de Bellas Artes Attend a performance here if you can. The theatre itself is a work of art. The colorful Ballet Folklórico usually performs Wednesdays and Sunday nights at 8:30 pm as well as Sunday mornings at 9:30 am.

Plaza Garibaldi *(Eje Central and Honduras, Centro)* is the place to go for traditional mariachi music. Mariachis are the guys you see in the tight-fitting suits decorated with metal studs and embroidery, and wearing wide sombreros. The image and the sound are associated with Mexico worldwide. They perform at birthday parties, weddings and political rallies; they are the ultimate expression of joyful national pride. Groups usually include guitars, violins and trumpets.

At Plaza Garibaldi musical mayhem reigns as people hire musicians to sing their favorite songs, with many groups playing at once. It is a unique sonic experience. There are bars and restaurants surrounding the area (some of which can be surprisingly expensive, so check prices before you order), but just strolling around the plaza is a quintessential Mexico City experience. Be careful with your wallets and pocketbooks.

Zinco Jazz Club *(Motolinia 20, near Cinco de Mayo, Centro, tel. 5512-3369, www.zincojazz.com)* This late night club (opens 10 pm) in the cellar of an Art-Deco building features the best jazz musicians in town. Price varies according to event. Also good is Blue Monk Jazz Club, (Bahía de San Hipólito 51, north of Polanco) www.bluemonkjazz.com

Mamá Rumba *(Locations in Roma, Polanco and San Angel, www.mamarumba.com.mx)* These popular clubs are welcoming places for latin dancing. Sometimes bands are even imported from Cuba. Free Salsa classes are offered afternoons.

La Bodega *(Calle Amsterdam at Popocatepetl, Colonia Condesa, www.labodega.com.mx)* You can eat, drink, listen to live Cuban music and dance at this comfortable and unpretentious bar/restaurant set in an old house. There is also a small theater upstairs with performers such as the eccentric songstress Astrid Hadad, known as "the Mexican Bette Midler" (check her out at *www.astridhadad.com*). Closed Sundays.

Mariachis playing at a restaurant in Plaza Garibaldi.

The American Legion *(Celaya 25, Condesa)* The formerly sleepy old Legion house (featuring a great Deco interior) has become a local hangout at night.

Art Openings Go to an art opening. Look in *Tiempo Libre* magazine under the *Museos y Galerias* section, where there are special listings for *Inauguraciones* (Openings). Galleries listed in the Polanco, Condesa and Roma sections of this book, as well as any of the major museums, will be likely to have fun and interesting openings.

Cinema Mexico City is a great movie town. There are numerous festivals—keep an eye out for posters at bus stops. Weekly listings are found in *Tiempo Libre* magazine, but they are arranged by theater chain, so it helps to know which theaters are near you. In the Centro look for listings under Cinemex Palacio Chino, Cinemex Real Cinema and Cinepolis Diana. In Colonia Condesa, it´s the Cinemex Plaza Insurgentes or Cinemex WTC, Colonia Roma has the Cinemex Cuauhtemoc, and in Polanco, look for the Cinemex Casa de Arte. The Zona Rosa has a Cinopolis at Reforma 222. Some theaters of the Cinepolis chain offer VIP salons, where you can relax in wide reclining chairs as waiters serve sushi—the tickets cost twice as much but it's worth it.

The Cineteca Nacional *(Avenida Mexico-Coyoacan 389, near Rio Churobusco — take a taxi or walk from Metro Coyoacán)* at the northern edge of Coyoacán is the place to be for serious cinephiles. They show an interesting mix of international films, new and old, in a 7-theater complex with bookstore and café. *www.cinetecanacional.net*

Gay Night Life

Gay travellers will generally find Mexico a comfortable place to visit. Mexicans are tolerant and apparently easy-going about sexuality, in spite of the force of machismo and the Catholic Church. Mexican culture is slowly recognizing its own sexual diversity - gay marriage is now legal in the Federal District as well as some states. Within families a policy of "don't ask, don't tell" often prevails, yet in the city it is not unusual to see same-sex couples walking hand-in-hand or even kissing in public.

Check out New Yorker-turned Chilango Michael Parker's **Gay Guide to Mexico City:** *www.scribd.com/doc/120513393/ LGBT-Guide-Mexico-City,* and for info all over *Mexico: www.gaymexicomap. com*

Tiempo Libre magazine offers listings of bars and discos (constantly changing) but there are a few old standbys that are always entertaining. In the Zona Rosa gay life centers around Calle Amberes near Reforma with several bars, restaurants and stores, generally catering to an under-30 crowd. Lipstick and Cabaret-Tito are among the most popular night spots here. **Nicho Bears & Bar** at Londres 182 is a friendly place open to bears and non-bears alike.

In the Centro Calle Republica de Cuba is where it's happening. **El Oasis** and **Viena** *(Republica de Cuba near Eje Central)* are relaxed cantinas with friendly ambience and neon-light decor. On weekends there is a floor show at Oasis that might even include a gay mariachi or waiters doing a striptease. **Marrakech**, down the block, is mixed and attracts a young hipster crowd. If you are looking for a gay experience that is truly Mexican, head to this street.

In La Condesa try **Tom's Leather Bar** *(Insurgentes 357 near Michoacán).* Hardly anybody wears leather in this very popular bar, in fact most are yuppies. It has beautiful, uninhibited go-go boys after 11pm. Best nights are Tuesday, Friday and Saturday; closed Mondays.

Sodome *(Mariano Escobedo 716, near the Camino Real hotel)* Anzures, is Mexico's only well appointed European-style sauna.

There are fewer choices for gay women in Mexico City—some bars have a special night for lesbians. Check weekly listings in Tiempo Libre and its website: www.tiempolibre.com.mx

LUCHA LIBRE

Lucha libre is that curious form of Mexican wrestling in which men, and occasionally women, dress in flashy Las Vegas style costumes and horror movie masks and proceed to stomp, throw, bend, crush, squeeze, and mangle one another around a ring, while the crowd roars its approval.

I confess I've never quite understood the allure of it all. But I recognize that the sport—if that's the right word—is extremely popular here and is definitely an international symbol of Mexican culture.

The memory of my first lucha libre experience is of the audience more than the wrestlers. It was very much a family event; people of all ages, even babies, were there. Everyone seemed to be in motion, gesturing toward the ring, screaming at the wrestlers, hopping up and down the aisles.

The lady in front of me looked like somebody's sweet old grandmother, or the woman who sells tortillas at my local market. That is, until she stood up and started screaming at the top of her lungs "Mátalo!, mátalo!" ("Kill him, kill him"). Something about the wrestling match seemed to unleash a base animal instinct, although I never worried that it would pass beyond the verbal.

Once, on a visit to New York City, my old home town, I was riding the subway when I witnessed an altercation between two women. It appeared that one of them bumped the other with her elbow.

Anger flared quickly. The scene reached its grand finale as one woman sneered, "You're a worthless piece of shit!" Turning up the volume, her adversary spit out the last line: "YOU'RE a worthless piece of shit!"

No one else in the subway seemed to notice, or care—just another day underground. I watched in disbelief as these two people, having met only 90 seconds ago before, descended the ladder of civilized behavior to its lowest rung—in public no less!

It's hard to imagine such a thing happening in Mexico City. I find Mexicans to be generally polite, kind, and courteous. In fact, in all the years I've lived here I can only recall two incidents in which I saw people raising their voices in anger to one another. Both cases involved damaged cars, so at least there seemed to be a good reason for it.

Does this mean that Mexicans are calmer by nature than New Yorkers? Or do they just save their screaming until they get home or attend a lucha libre match? Maybe the mayor of New York should build a lucha libre arena in Central Park to find out.

Where to see it:

If you're interested in attending a match, the two main venues are listed below. Both websites are in Spanish only—click *cartelera* to see current events.

Arena Mexico *(Dr. Lavista 197, Colonia Doctores, www.arenamexico.com.mx)*

Arena Coliseo *(Peru 77, Centro, www.cmll.com)*

You can buy tickets at the door of both arenas, but they sometimes sell out. You might try *ticketmaster.com.mx* and type in the words 'lucha libre' where it says BUSCAR.

WHERE TO SHOP

Sanborns This chain of stores is mentioned throughout the book, and you will see them all over Mexico. It is very handy for books, magazine, pharmacy items, chocolate, and a light meal. You can always find clean bathrooms and an ATM. Some are open all night.

Fonart *(Juarez 89, Centro and also Patriotismo 691, Mixcoac)* The Fundación Nacional de Artesanias is a chain of stores throughout the country selling craftwork from all regions of Mexico. There is a good selection of ceramics, glass, weaving, basketry, woodwork, and more at reasonable prices. (www.fonart.gob.mx)

Victor *(Isabel la Católica 97)* is a decades-old family-run store offering an eclectic selection of high quality Mexican handicrafts and silver jewelry. You'll find lots of good 'stocking stuffers' here.

Museo de Arte Popular *(Independencia and Revillagigedo, Centro)*. The gift store at this excellent museum has a good selection of crafts at reasonable prices. All profits go to the artisans.

La Ciudadela *(Balderas at Emilio Donde, Centro)*. This market has dozens of stalls selling traditional handmade items at good prices. You will find hammocks, glassware, baskets, sombreros, textiles, silver, and lots more good things to bring home. It's the best of the various tourist markets around town. On Saturday afternoons there is outdoor dancing at the Plaza de Danzón nearby.

Mata Ortiz pottery from Chihuahua on display at FONART.

Mercado de Artesanías *(Londres 154, Zona Rosa)* Similar to La Ciudadela, but smaller, and claustrophobic. But if you're looking for silver jewelry, this is the place.

Palacio de Máscaras *(Allende 84, between Honduras and Ecuador, Centro)* has more than 5000 masks (mostly new) from all parts of Mexico.

New Books Books are expensive in Mexico and, sadly, you don't see a lot of people reading. Ghandi is the largest bookseller with several locations. One is directly across from the Palacio de Bellas Artes (which also has its own good bookstore). The largest Ghandi is located at Miguel Ángel de Quevedo 128 near Avenida Universidad in Coyoacán.

Centro Cultural Bella Época *(Tamaulipas 202 at Benjamin Hill)* has a large, well-stocked bookstore, gallery, café, cinema, and children's play area housed in a smartly renovated art deco movie theater in Colonia Condesa.

Used Books Under the Volcano Books *(Celaya 25, Colonia Condesa)* has a small but savvy collection of used books in English.

In the Centro along Calle Donceles you'll find several stores selling used books in all languages.

Bazar del Sábado *(Plaza de San Jacinto, San Ángel)* This Saturday-only market features quality craft items by local artisans. It's a maze of little rooms with lots of surprises. Go before noon as it gets crowded.

Upscale Shopping Avenida President Masaryk in Polanco is where you will find the line-up of big name stores—Bulgari, Gucci, Fendi, etc. The Centro Comercial Antara (Antara mall), near the Soumaya Museum in Polanco, is the fanciest in town. The slick Centro Comercial Santa Fé on the far western edge of the city is the largest in Latin America. Two department store chains, Palacio de Hierro and Liverpool, have branches throughout the city; prices tend to be high as many items are imported.

FLEA MARKETS

While, like everywhere in the world, it's harder to find bargains these days, a stroll through a *mercado de pulgas* is a pleasant was to pass a Saturday or Sunday morning. And you never know what you'll find...

La Lagunilla Flea Market *(Reforma near Jaime Nuno, just north of Metro stop Garibaldi)* It is the best flea market in the city. Only on Sundays.

Cuauhtémoc Flea Market *(In the small park between Dr. Liceaga and Dr. Juan Navarro, just across from Jardín Pushkin in Colonia Roma)* Saturdays and Sundays, but some of the best vendors go to Lagunilla on Sundays

Portales Market (*Rumania between Libertad and Santa Cruz, near metro Portales*) is a scrappy affair, but treasures can be found. There's a big used furniture store nearby at Montes de Oca 391. Open daily, but best on weekends.

Plaza del Ángel (*Londres 161 and Hamburgo 150, Zona Rosa*) Saturday and Sunday flea market, more upscale than the others in town.

Alantigua, (*Guanajuato 133 near Jalapa in Colonia Roma*) is a junk/ furniture shop, open Monday, Wednesday, Friday only.

CULTURE:
ART, ARCHITECTURE, CRAFTS, MUSIC & FILM

ART

Pre-Hispanic Art

The most important art in
Mexico before the conquest
was made by the Olmecs on
the Gulf coast (1200 B.C.
to 1 A.D.), the Mayas in the
Yucatan (300 to 900A.D.),
and the Aztecs in the valley of
Mexico (1350 to 1521 A.D).
The culture of Teotihuacán
(100 to 700 A.D.), whose ruins lie 50km northeast of the city, stands
apart as a major influence on subsequent art, but not a direct ethnic
lineage. The best places to see this art are the Museo de Antropology,
the Museo del Templo Mayor, the Museo Dolores Olmedo, and the
Museo Anahuacalli.

Colonial Art

Mexico was a colony of Spain until 1821, and influences of art of this
period are mainly European in style and religious in content. Miguel
Cabrera and Juan Correa are painters from the 1700's whose work stands
out. The best places to see Colonial Art are the Museo Nacional, the
Museo del Carmen, the Museo Franz Mayer, and the Museo San Carlos.

Post-Independence Art

Although European influence still dominated the scene, a national
identity in Mexican art began to emerge in the 19th century. The
native landscapes of José Maria Velasco (1840-1912) are evocative and
proud. The popular black and white prints of José Guadalupe Posada
(1852-1913) used caricature and political satire as their tools, and his
skeletal images have become Mexican icons. The artist known as
Dr. Atl (1875-1964) painted landscapes (he was especially fond of

volcanos) noted for their intense, emotional color. You'll find examples of this art at the Museo Nacional.

The Muralist Movement

When things settled down after the 1910 Revolution, the government began a program of public mural painting to encourage awareness of Mexican heritage. The most famous muralist is Diego Rivera (1885-1957), perhaps better known now as the husband of Frida Kahlo. Two other important muralists are José Clement Orozco (1883-1949) and David Alfaro Siqueiros (1896-1974), whose works have a more strident political feel. Juan O'Gorman (also a noted architect) designed massive mosaic murals at the university. Rufino Tamayo is another important artist of this period who painted murals which incorporated more modern abstraction.

There are murals all over town, but some of the best places to visit are the Palacio Nacional, the Secretaría de Educación Pública and the Museo Mural Diego Rivera (these three have the best of Rivera); the Palacio de Bellas Artes and the Castillo de Chapultepec have murals by several artists.

Frida Kahlo

One tires quickly of the images slapped on t-shirts and shopping bags, but the almost-naive art of this doomed heroine retains its haunting power when you see it in person. The best collection is at the Museo Dolores Olmedo, but paintings are often out on loan to other museums. The Museo de Arte Moderno owns a few important paintings, but Frida's own house has mostly sketches and lesser works.

Contemporary Mexican Art

In the 1960's, a group of young artists including José Luis Cuevas and Francisco Toledo rebelled against the established mural movement forming La Ruptura, which dealt with current abstract concepts. Nowadays, much of what one sees in Mexico City art galleries looks like an imitation of New York or Berlin, trying hard to be cool, looking like too much time was spent in art school. However, a few artists have made names for themselves in the world art market. Gabriel Orozco stands out with his quirky sculptures and installations.

ARCHITECTURE

Pre-Hispanic Architecture

The scale model of Aztec Mexico City in the Museo de Antropología offers a teasing idea of the architecture, as do the ruins at the Templo Mayor—use your imagination here. Teotihuacán is the best place to see near-complete examples of pre-Hispanic architecture on the grandest scale.

Colonial Architecture

European grandeur arrived with the Spaniards, whose architectural legacy is strong in Mexico City. Flamboyant Baroque highlights include the main altar of the Catedral, the Palacio de Iturbide, and the Santo Domingo and Nuestra Señora del Pilar churches in the Centro. The best ensemble of neo-classic architecture surrounds the Plaza Manuel Tolsá by the Museo Nacional.

Porfiriato Architecture

Like Queen Victoria, the reign of President Porfirio Díaz (1876 to 1910) lasted long enough to claim its own architectural style. He left the stamp of Paris all over the country; the cast-iron bandstands one sees in towns all over Mexico date from this period. The finest architectural examples are the exterior of the Palacio de Bellas Artes, the Correo Mayor, and the residential architecture of Colonia Roma.

Art Deco

Aztec influence on deco design of the 1920's and 1930's gives it a unique look in Mexico. The interior of the Palacio de Bellas Artes is the supreme example of this style, and Colonia Condesa is one of the best-preserved art deco neighborhoods in the world.

Contemporary Architecture

Although Mexico City has its share of dull steel and glass boxes, there is also a strong element of theatrical flair to be found, such as the Museo Soumaya in Polanco. Examples of daring designs of high-rise commercial buildings can be seen along Reforma, Insurgentes Sur, and especially in the Santa Fe area at the western end of the city, which looks a bit like Tokyo. The Centro Nacional de las Artes near Coyoacán is an impressive complex of modern buildings by various architects. The prize winning José Vasconcelos Library (next to Buenavista Station) is worth a visit.

SIX ARCHITECTS WHO CHANGED THE FACE OF MEXICO CITY

Manuel Tolsá (1757-1816) Born in Spain, Tolsá introduced the classic, academic style to Mexico. He completed work on the Cathedral, and graced the city with buildings such as the Palacio de Minería and the Palacio de Buenavista (today the Museo de San Carlos), with its lovely oval courtyard. His equestrian statue of Charles IV in front of the Palacio de Minería is a symbol of the city.

Juan O'Gorman (1905-1982) was a painter and architect. He was a proponent of functionalist architecture, best appreciated in the studios of Diego Rivera and Frida Kahlo in San Ángel. But his most famous work is the iconic, mosaic-clad library at Mexico's national university, UNAM. His panoramic historical murals at Chapultepec Castle and his self-portrait at the Museo de Arte Moderno are outstanding examples of his highly detailed painting style. His later art became mannered, taking on a hippy, acid-trip look.

Luis Barragán (1902-1988). Barragán's output was small, but his influence was great. He combined a minimalist esthetic with the colors and textures of traditional Mexican design. Anyone seriously interested in architecture should visit his house and studio and his convent in Tlalpan. His famous Torres de Satellite often appear on tourist brochures for Mexico City.

Ricardo Legoretta (1931-2011) was Barragán's most distinguished disciple, although his work lacks the spiritual element of the master. The Camino Real Hotel, Plaza Juárez, and El Papalote children's museum are among his most famous works.

Pedro Ramirez Vásquez (1919-2013). Known as 'the father of Mexican architecture', he is responsible for such works as the magnificent Museum of Anthropology, the flashy Basilica of the Virgin of Guadalupe, and the spaceship-like Museum of Modern Art, as well as dozens of government buildings, markets, and museums throughout the country.

Francisco Serrano (1900-1982) created some of the finest examples of art deco and modernist architecture in the city: the Edifico Basurto in the Condesa and Pasaje Polanco in Polanco are two standouts.

The Torres de Satélite ("Satélite Towers") designed by renowned Mexican architect Luis Barragán.

CRAFTS

Mexican artisans are famous worldwide as potters, weavers, jewelers, wood carvers, mask makers, and metal workers. Spanish priests advanced the cause of Mexican craftsmanship by organizing indigenous guilds and encouraging trade, and the government continues its support. In many places, the quality of crafts has fallen with the influence of mass-produced items, but good things are still being made. The finest craft regions are in the states of Oaxaca and Michoacán. **The Museo de Arte Popular** has the best collection in town, and a good gift store, too. **FONART** stores, **Victor**, and the **Ciudadela market** are the best places in Mexico City to shop for crafts.

MUSIC

Traditional Mexican music has deep roots in indigenous music, as well as European popular song, flamenco, and even German beer hall bands. While current global trends are what you will often hear in the street, tradition dies hard and many performers keep the flame burning: even teenagers know the old songs. Ghandi Bookstores and Mix-Up Music Stores are the best place to find commercial CD's. Libreria Bella Época in Condesa has a good selection.

Ranchera, or country music, encompasses folk, mariachi, norteña, banda, jarocho, and a host of other idioms. The era of "Great Divas and Divos" of ranchera is past (think Sinatra and Clooney) but their recordings are widely available. Lola Beltran, "La Reina de la Canción Ranchera" sang definitive versions of classic rancheras; when she died, people from all walks of life lined up for blocks to see her laid out in state in Bellas Artes. Runner up was Amalia Mendoza, whose best-known hit was "Amarga Navidad," or "Bitter Christmas," which ends with lots of melodramatic weeping and wailing. Other great voices  were Lucha Villa, Yolanda Del Rio and Rocío Durcal. Chavela Vargas has at last received her due fame, thanks to some promotion by Pedro Almodóvar, and she has become a willing lesbian icon. Pop singer Ana

Gabriel, with a distinctive gravelly voice, has a wonderful album of traditional music, Joyas de Dos Siglos, accompanying herself on guitar. Linda Ronstadt has made a big impression with her versions of classic songs on three albums, all good, and she pays tribute to the greats who preceded her. The original "Mexican Piaf" was Lucha Reyes, the first woman to record ranchera music.

The great male singers of the genre are Pedro Vargas, Javier Solis and Jose Alfredo Jiménez, also a beloved composer. Pedro Infante and Jorge Negrete are golden-voiced crooners who were also big matinee idols of the 1940's. Alejandro Fernández, who has become even more famous than his father Vicente, is a current heartthrob with a beautiful voice.

Bolero, or "ballad" music is a style closer to classic American pop, "Bésame Mucho" being the most well-known example of a bolero. Songwriter and performer, "el músico-poeta," **Agustín Lara** wrote thousands of songs, including "Granada," that are still known and sung. His muse, **Toña la Negra,** was the best interpreter of his music (Ronstadt pays tribute to her). Her recordings from the 1950's are the best. Few in Mexico seems to know that **Eydie Gormé**, who recorded a pair of wonderful albums with the Trio los Panchos in the 1960's, is a gringa, so minimal is her accent. Today, **Eugenia León** who possesses an extraordinary, large voice, has inherited the mantel of Queen Diva in just about every genre; her Tirana album is the best. Opera stars Olivia Gorra and Fernando de la Mora have also done a good deal of bolero albums: look for her Pecadora and his Boleros. The L.A. based group **Los Lobos** recorded an exemplary album of folk music, La Pistola y el Corazón. Amparo Ochoa was a chronicler of traditional folk songs and corridas, songs that tell stories. Several younger singers have revived interest in more traditional folk styles: **Lila Downs, Georgina Meneses** and **Susana Harp**.

Nowadays there is an active pop scene; while many genres are imitations of North American pop, some alternative artists to look out for are Julieta Venegas, Café Tacuba.

There is a rich body of Mexican "classical" music, from localized European styles of the colonial era, to distinguished modern composers of the 20th century such as Silvestre Revueltas, Carlos Chávez and Manuel M. Ponce who incorporated elements of folk styles into their work.

FILM

The Golden Age of Mexican Cinema

Since the late 1930's, when Spain and Argentina stopped producing much cinema due to political strife, Mexico has been the leading producer of Spanish language film (and later television). The industry's "Golden Age" was the 1940's and '50's, when many films were made either in genres similar to those of Hollywood, or styles peculiar to Mexico, such as the ranchera (musical western) and rumbera films. Many of these classics are available in inexpensive DVD versions, some with English subtitles.

Santa *(1931)*
The first sound film made in Mexico from the best-selling novel by Fernando Gamboa. Agustín Lara's song of the same name is sung to accompany an extraordinary brothel scene. It was filmed partly in Colonia Condesa, and was the first of a genre of "good girl gone bad" movies.

La Mujer del Puerto *(1933)*
Good girl becomes whore, through no fault of her own...starring the fabulous Andrea Palma the "Mexican Dietrich."

Allá en el Rancho Grande *(1936)*
The archetypal comedia ranchera, a genre popular until the 1990's when Hollywood and free trade practically killed off the Mexican cinema industry.

Distinto Amanecer (Another Dawn) *(1943)*
One of the greatest film noirs ever made, rivaling Casablanca—once again starring Andrea Palma and making Pedro Armendariz a star. The train station finale gives one goose bumps!

Maria Candelaria *(1943)*
The first product of the great team of director Emilio "El Indio" Fernández and cinematographer Gabriel Figueroa, and Dolores Del Río's return to Mexican Cinema after a long stay in Hollywood. Made in conjunction with intellectuals and artists (including Diego Rivera) to promote the nobility of Mexican indigenous culture. Filmed on location in the "floating gardens of Xochimilco" (where everyone can tell you, to this day, which canals were used as locations).

Enamorada *(1946)*
María Felix was Latin America's greatest star, not well known in the USA as she never worked in Hollywood. This is her best film, another Fernández/Figueroa collaboration, and  a prototype of the Revolutionary film genre. The scene where Felix is serenaded and the camera zooms up to her eyes is justly famous.

Salón México *(1946)*
Another Fernández/Figueroa collaboration, and a noir classic, which made the late Marga Lopez a star. Another long-suffering prostitute story, beautifully filmed and all taking place in Mexico City at night (in the rain, naturally).

Los Olvidados *(1950)*
Filmed on location in Mexico City (including Colonia Roma and the Centro), Luis Buñuel's superb portrait of the struggling classes was banned shortly after its premier, offending some for showing Mexico in a bad light. In 2005 it was the first film to be named by UNESCO as part of their Universal Cultural Patrimony program.

Nosotros Los Pobres *(1948)*
Starring the great singer/actor Pedro Infante, who created the archetype Pepe el Toro, the urban working class hero. It was an attempt to depict and dignify the working class poor of Mexico City, several years before the more sophisticated (and pessimistic) Los Olvidados was made. This is the best known and beloved film in all of Mexican cinema, like It's A Wonderful Life is in the USA.

Aventurera *(1949)*
The best known in a series of lurid rumbera films, another genre peculiar to Mexican Cinema which combines noir and campy musical numbers, and usually takes place in the underworld of nightclubs and gangsters. It stars over-the-top Cuban actress Ninón Sevilla.

RECOMMENDED READING

History of the Conquest of New Spain by Bernal Díaz del Castillo—an amazing description of Tenochtitlán by one of Cortés' followers.

Life in Mexico by Frances Calderon De La Barca—Life in New Spain in the early 19th century vividly portrayed.

Sor Juana's Love Poems by Sor Juana Inés de la Cruz. Mexico's great 17th century poet.

The Underdogs by Mariano Azuela. Mexico's first novel of the revolution.

Pedro Páramo by Juan Rulfo who had a major influence in the development of magical realism.

Where the Air is Clear by Carlos Fuentes is a modern urban epic by Mexico's best-known contemporary novelist.

The Labyrinth of Solitude by Octavio Paz will give you an insight into the Mexican national character.

La Capital: The Biography of Mexico City by Jonathan Kandell is a fun and informative read and a great general history.

Frida: A Biography of Frida Kahlo by Hayden Herrera. Even if you haven't been caught up by "Frida-mania," this bio is worth reading as it paints a vivid portrait of the Golden Age of Mexican culture of the 1920's-1950's.

First Stop in the New World, by David Lida, is a contemporary look at the underbelly of Mexico City by a long-time aficionado of urban life.

The Treasure of the Sierra Madre by Englishman B. Traven who wrote about Mexico like an insider. If you can read Spanish, his Canasta de cuentos mexicanos is superb, and funny, although his Treasure of Sierra Madre is more famous.

CENTRO HISTORICO

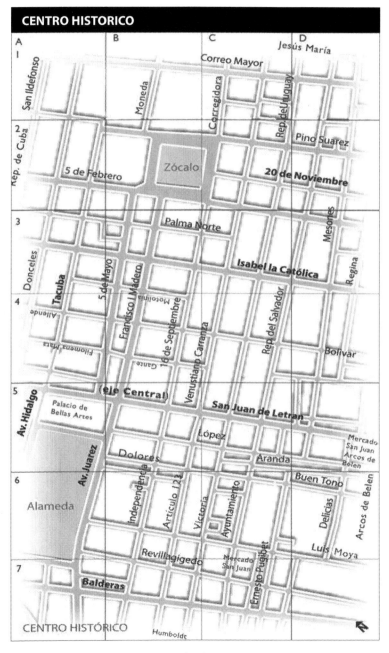

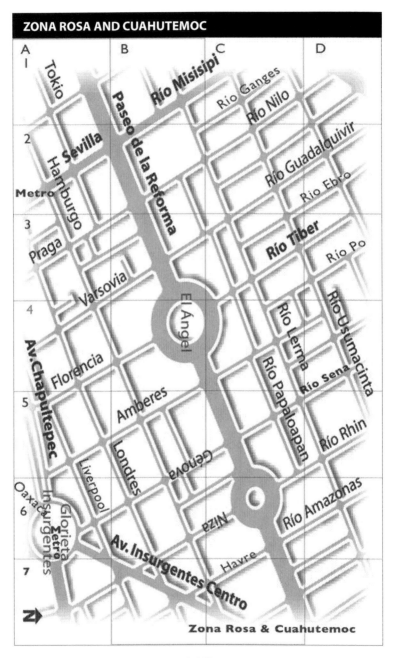

ZONA ROSA AND CUAHUTEMOC

Zona Rosa & Cuahutemoc

POLANCO

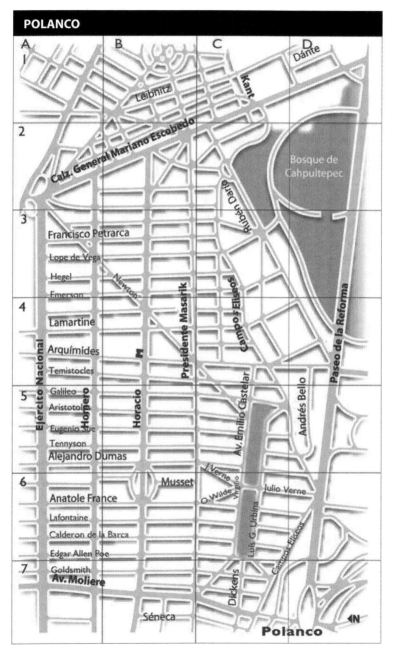

SAN ANGEL

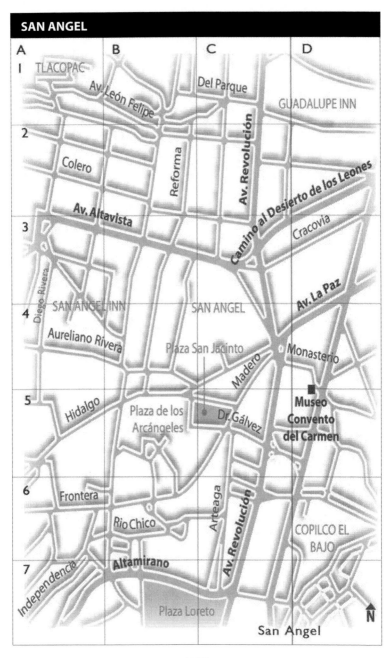

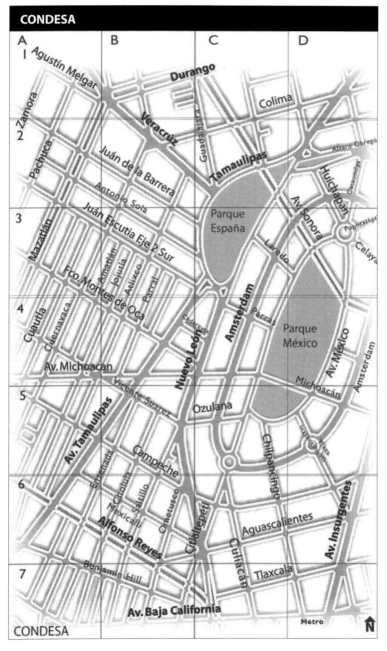

CONDESA

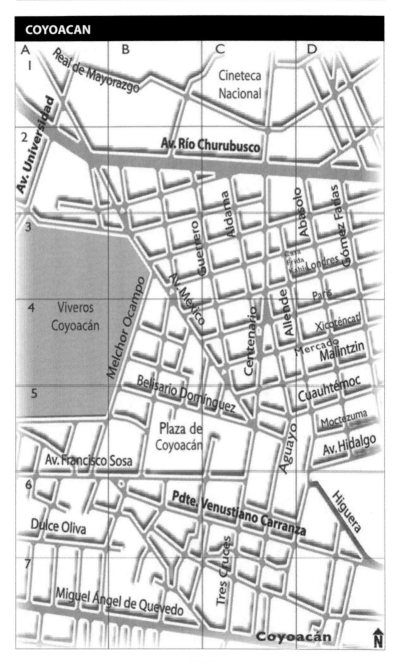

COYOACAN

ABOUT THE AUTHOR

Jim Johnston was born in New York City and grew up in the woods of New Hampshire. After studying architecture at the University of Virginia and graphic design at the School of Visual Arts, he worked as a professional artist in New York City for 27 years before moving full-time to Mexico in 1997, where he continues working as an artist and writer. He resides in Mexico City with his partner Nicholas Gilman.

Visit my blog: www.mexicocitydf.com
for updates and more.

Website: www.jimjohnstonart.com

Follow me on Facebook at 'Mexico City: an Opinionated Guide' and 'Estudio Tonalá'

Reader's comments and suggestions are welcome by email: jimjohnstonart@gmail.com

Index

A

B

C

N

Reader Comments

"We have been to DF over 20 times and this guide gave us ideas for another 20 visits. We would give this book to anyone considering a visit to DF, whether it's their first visit or their fiftieth."

"Great guide book! It's like visiting an old friend that takes you on a tour of his city."

"I seldom read travel books from cover to cover but this one I did since its focus is architecture, there were always gems to seek out on our daily path."

"My husband and I just returned from five days in Mexico City and relied heavily on Jim Johnston's guide. His emphasis on food, art, and design spoke directly to our interests. We loved his tips on street food, a topic most guides completely ignore. We are already planning a return trip and this guide will certainly come with us."

"What a delightful book about one of my favorite cities and cultures! Instead of flipping to the glossary to find say, "museums" or "restaurants" and then reading a brief note of the address followed by a short description, I found that once I had begun reading the Introduction I simply couldn't put it down and just read it straight through until the end."

"This book shares special information not found in other guides and is written with a personal passion that will really add value and authenticity to your trip."

"This one takes you off the beaten track and leads you through tours of less frequented neighborhoods. Its like having a (very well informed) local right there with you."

"The book is a pleaure to read - he has a keen eye and his passion for DF is infectious."

"I bought several travel guides before I went to Mexico City. This was the only one that I took with me every day before I left the hotel."

" Maybe most important is that the ethic and personality of the author come through, revealing him as someone you would like to know - and you will, with this book."

"This is not a typical travel guide. I live in Mexico and would never know the "real" Mexico City without this one. The author really loves this place and this guide is a gift to anyone who wants to explore the best kept secrets of this intense and marvelous city."

"If you've ever wished that you had a friend to guide you around Mexico City, rejoice! You've got one in Jim Johnston. Reading his 'opinionated guide' is like having a trusted pal steer you through a maze by gently taking your elbow and whispering in your ear. He's got a great a sense of humor and offers very useful and detailed info that will help you have a special and memorable trip."

Made in the USA
Middletown, DE
22 February 2018